PENGUIN PLAYS

A VIEW FROM THE BRIDGE

AND

ALL MY SONS

Arthur Miller was born in New York City in 1915 and studied at the University of Michigan. His plays include *Death of a Salesman* (1949), *The Crucible* (1953), *A Memory of Two Mondays* (1955), *After the Fall* (1963), *Incident at Vichy* (1964) and *The Price* (1968). His most recent play is *The Creation of the World and Other Business* (1972). He has also written three novels, *Focus* (1945), *The Misfits*, which was filmed in 1960 and *In Russia* (1969). He has twice won the New York Drama Critics' Award, and in 1949 he was awarded the Pulitzer Prize.

ARTHUR MILLER

A View from the Bridge
All My Sons

PENGUIN BOOKS

Penguin Books Ltd, Harmondsworth, Middlesex, England
Penguin Books, 625 Madison Avenue, New York, New York 10022, U.S.A.
Penguin Books Australia Ltd, Ringwood, Victoria, Australia
Penguin Books Canada Ltd, 41 Steelcase Road West, Markham, Ontario, Canada
Penguin Books (N.Z.) Ltd, 182–190 Wairau Road, Auckland 10, New Zealand

—

A View from the Bridge first published 1955
First published in Great Britain by the Cresset Press 1957
Copyright © Arthur Miller, 1955

All My Sons first published 1947
First published in Great Britain by the Cresset Press 1958
Copyright © Arthur Miller, 1947

—

Published in Penguin Books, 1961
Reprinted in 1963, 1965, 1967, 1968, 1969, 1970, 1971, 1972, 1973,
1974, 1975, 1976 (twice)

—

Made and printed in Great Britain
by Hazell Watson & Viney Ltd,
Aylesbury, Bucks
Set in Monotype Bembo

All applications for a licence to perform this play must be made
either to the International Famous Agency Ltd, 11–12 Hanover
Street, London W1 (for professional performance), or to the
English Theatre Guild, 52 Dean Street, London W1 (for
repertory and amateur performance).

Contents

A VIEW FROM THE BRIDGE

ALL MY SONS

A VIEW FROM THE BRIDGE

A VIEW FROM THE BRIDGE

*First performed at the Comedy Theatre, London, on 11 October 1956,
with the following cast:*

LOUIS	Richard Harris
MIKE	Norman Mitchell
ALFIERI	Michael Gwynn
EDDIE	Anthony Quayle
CATHERINE	Mary Ure
BEATRICE	Megs Jenkins
MARCO	Ian Bannen
TONY	Ralph Nossek
RODOLPHO	Brian Bedford
FIRST IMMIGRATION OFFICER	John Stone
SECOND IMMIGRATION OFFICER	Colin Rix
MR LIPARI	Mervyn Blake
MRS LIPARI	Catherine Willmer
'SUBMARINE'	Peter Jones

CHARACTERS OF THE PLAY

LOUIS	
MIKE	FIRST IMMIGRATION OFFICER
ALFIERI	SECOND IMMIGRATION OFFICER
EDDIE	MR LIPARI
CATHERINE	MRS LIPARI
BEATRICE	TWO 'SUBMARINES'
MARCO	NEIGHBOURS
TONY	
RODOLPHO	

ACT ONE

The street and house-front of a tenement building. The front is skeletal entirely. The main acting area is the living-room–dining-room of Eddie's apartment. It is a worker's flat, clean, sparse, homely. There is a rocker down front; a round dining-table at centre, with chairs; and a portable phonograph.

At back are a bedroom door and an opening to the kitchen; none of these interiors is seen.

At the right, forestage, a desk. This is Mr Alfieri's law office.

There is also a telephone booth. This is not used until the last scenes, so it may be covered or left in view.

A stairway leads up to the apartment, and then farther up to the next storey, which is not seen.

Ramps, representing the street, run upstage and off to right and left. As the curtain rises, LOUIS and MIKE, longshoremen, are pitching coins against the building at left.

A distant foghorn blows.

> [*Enter* ALFIERI, *a lawyer in his fifties turning grey; he is portly, good-humoured, and thoughtful. The two pitchers nod to him as he passes. He crosses the stage to his desk, removes his hat, runs his fingers through his hair, and grinning, speaks to the audience.*]

ALFIERI: You wouldn't have known it, but something amusing has just happened. You see how uneasily they nod to me? That's because I am a lawyer. In this neighbourhood to meet a lawyer or a priest on the street is unlucky. We're only thought of in connexion with disasters, and they'd rather not get too close.

I often think that behind that suspicious little nod of theirs lie three thousand years of distrust. A lawyer means the law, and in Sicily, from where their fathers came, the law has not been a friendly idea since the Greeks were beaten.

I am inclined to notice the ruins in things, perhaps because I was born in Italy. ... I only came here when I was twenty-five. In those days, Al Capone, the greatest Carthaginian of all, was learning his trade on these pavements, and Frankie Yale himself was cut precisely in half by a machine-gun on the corner of Union Street, two blocks away. Oh, there were many here who were justly shot by unjust men. Justice is very important here.

But this is Red Hook, not Sicily. This is the slum that faces the bay on the seaward side of Brooklyn Bridge. This is the gullet of New York swallowing the tonnage of the world. And now we are quite civilized, quite American. Now we settle for half, and I like it better. I no longer keep a pistol in my filing cabinet.

And my practice is entirely unromantic.

My wife has warned me, so have my friends; they tell me the people in this neighbourhood lack elegance, glamour. After all, who have I dealt with in my life? Longshoremen and their wives, and fathers, and grandfathers, compensation cases, evictions, family squabbles – the petty troubles of the poor – and yet ... every few years there is still a case, and as the parties tell me what the trouble is, the flat air in my office suddenly washes in with the green scent of the sea, the dust in this air is blown away and the thought comes that in some Caesar's year, in Calabria perhaps or on the cliff at Syracuse, another lawyer, quite differently dressed, heard the same complaint and sat there as powerless as I, and watched it run its bloody course.

[EDDIE *has appeared and has been pitching coins with the men and is highlighted among them. He is forty – a husky, slightly overweight longshoreman.*]

This one's name was Eddie Carbone, a longshoreman working the docks from Brooklyn Bridge to the breakwater where the open sea begins.

[ALFIERI *walks into darkness.*]

EDDIE [*moving up steps into doorway*]: Well, I'll see ya, fellas.

[CATHERINE *enters from kitchen, crosses down to window, looks out.*]

LOUIS: You workin' tomorrow?

EDDIE: Yeah, there's another day yet on that ship. See ya, Louis.

[EDDIE *goes into the house, as light rises in the apartment.* CATHERINE *is waving to* LOUIS *from the window and turns to him.*]

CATHERINE: Hi, Eddie!

[EDDIE *is pleased and therefore shy about it; he hangs up his cap and jacket.*]

EDDIE: Where you goin' all dressed up?

CATHERINE [*running her hands over her skirt*]: I just got it. You like it?

EDDIE: Yeah, it's nice. And what happened to your hair?

CATHERINE: You like it? I fixed it different. [*Calling to kitchen*] He's here, B.!

EDDIE: Beautiful. Turn around, lemme see in the back. [*She turns for him.*] Oh, if your mother was alive to see you now! She wouldn't believe it.

CATHERINE: You like it, huh?

EDDIE: You look like one of them girls that went to college. Where you goin'?

CATHERINE [*taking his arm*]: Wait'll B. comes in, I'll tell you something. Here, sit down. [*She is walking him to the arm-chair. Calling offstage*] Hurry up, will you, B.?

EDDIE [*sitting*]: What's goin' on?

CATHERINE: I'll get you a beer, all right?

EDDIE: Well, tell me what happened. Come over here, talk to me.

CATHERINE: I want to wait till B. comes in. [*She sits on her heels beside him.*] Guess how much we paid for the skirt.

EDDIE: I think it's too short, ain't it?

CATHERINE [*standing*]: No! not when I stand up.

EDDIE: Yeah, but you gotta sit down sometimes.

CATHERINE: Eddie, it's the style now. [*She walks to show him.*] I mean, if you see me walkin' down the street –

EDDIE: Listen, you been givin' me the willies the way you walk down the street, I mean it.

CATHERINE: Why?

EDDIE: Catherine, I don't want to be a pest, but I'm tellin' you you're walkin' wavy.

CATHERINE: I'm walkin' wavy?

EDDIE: Now don't aggravate me, Katie, you are walkin' wavy! I don't like the looks they're givin' you in the candy store. And with them new high heels on the sidewalk – clack, clack, clack. The heads are turnin' like windmills.

CATHERINE: But those guys look at all the girls, you know that.

EDDIE: You ain't 'all the girls'.

CATHERINE [*almost in tears because he disapproves*]: What do you want me to do? You want me to –

EDDIE: Now don't get mad, kid.

CATHERINE: Well, I don't know what you want from me.

EDDIE: Katie, I promised your mother on her deathbed. I'm responsible for you. You're a baby, you don't understand these things. I mean like when you stand here by the window, wavin' outside.

CATHERINE: I was wavin' to Louis!

EDDIE: Listen, I could tell you things about Louis which you wouldn't wave to him no more.

CATHERINE [*trying to joke him out of his warning*]: Eddie, I wish there was one guy you couldn't tell me things about!

EDDIE: Catherine, do me a favour, will you? You're getting

to be a big girl now, you gotta keep yourself more, you can't be so friendly, kid. [*Calls*] Hey, B., what're you doin' in there? [*To* CATHERINE] Get her in here, will you? I got news for her.

CATHERINE [*starting out*]: What?

EDDIE: Her cousins landed.

CATHERINE [*clapping her hands together*]: No! [*She turns instantly and starts for the kitchen.*] B.! Your cousins!

[BEATRICE *enters, wiping her hands with a towel.*]

BEATRICE [*in the face of* CATHERINE'*s shout*]: What?

CATHERINE: Your cousins got in!

BEATRICE [*astounded, turns to* EDDIE]: What are you talkin' about? Where?

EDDIE: I was just knockin' off work before and Tony Bereli come over to me; he says the ship is in the North River.

BEATRICE [– *her hands are clasped at her breast; she seems half in fear, half in unutterable joy*]: They're all right?

EDDIE: He didn't see them yet, they're still on board. But as soon as they get off he'll meet them. He figures about ten o'clock they'll be here.

BEATRICE [*sits, almost weak from tension*]: And they'll let them off the ship all right? That's fixed, heh?

EDDIE: Sure, they give them regular seamen papers and they walk off with the crew. Don't worry about it, B., there's nothin' to it. Couple of hours they'll be here.

BEATRICE: What happened? They wasn't supposed to be till next Thursday.

EDDIE: I don't know; they put them on any ship they can get them on. Maybe the other ship they was supposed to take there was some danger – What you cryin' about?

BEATRICE [*astounded and afraid*]: I'm – I just – I can't believe it! I didn't even buy a new tablecloth; I was gonna wash the walls –

EDDIE: Listen, they'll think it's a millionaire's house compared to the way they live. Don't worry about the walls. They'll be thankful. [*To* CATHERINE] Whyn't you run down buy a tablecloth. Go ahead, here. [*He is reaching into his pocket.*]

CATHERINE: There's no stores open now.

EDDIE [*to* BEATRICE]: You was gonna put a new cover on the chair.

BEATRICE: I know – well, I thought it was gonna be next week! I was gonna clean the walls, I was gonna wax the floors. [*She stands disturbed.*]

CATHERINE [*pointing upward*]: Maybe Mrs Dondero upstairs –

BEATRICE [*of the tablecloth*]: No, hers is worse than this one. [*Suddenly*] My God, I don't even have nothin' to eat for them! [*She starts for the kitchen.*]

EDDIE [*reaching out and grabbing her arm*]: Hey, hey! Take it easy.

BEATRICE: No, I'm just nervous, that's all. [*To* CATHERINE] I'll make the fish.

EDDIE: You're savin' their lives, what're you worryin' about the tablecloth? They probably didn't see a tablecloth in their whole life where they come from.

BEATRICE [*looking into his eyes*]: I'm just worried about you, that's all I'm worried.

EDDIE: Listen, as long as they know where they're gonna sleep.

BEATRICE: I told them in the letters. They're sleepin' on the floor.

EDDIE: Beatrice, all I'm worried about is you got such a heart that I'll end up on the floor with you, and they'll be in our bed.

BEATRICE: All right, stop it.

EDDIE: Because as soon as you see a tired relative, I end up on the floor.

BEATRICE: When did you end up on the floor?

EDDIE: When your father's house burned down I didn't end up on the floor?

BEATRICE: Well, their house burned down!

EDDIE: Yeah, but it didn't keep burnin' for two weeks!

BEATRICE: All right, look, I'll tell them to go someplace else. [*She starts into the kitchen.*]

EDDIE: Now wait a minute. Beatrice! [*She halts. He goes to her.*] I just don't want you bein' pushed around, that's all. You got too big a heart. [*He touches her hand.*] What're you so touchy?

BEATRICE: I'm just afraid if it don't turn out good you'll be mad at me.

EDDIE: Listen, if everybody keeps his mouth shut, nothin' can happen. They'll pay for their board.

BEATRICE: Oh, I told them.

EDDIE: Then what the hell. [*Pause. He moves.*] It's an honour, B. I mean it. I was just thinkin' before, comin' home, suppose my father didn't come to this country, and I was starvin' like them over there ... and I had people in America could keep me a couple of months? The man would be honoured to lend me a place to sleep.

BEATRICE [– *there are tears in her eyes. She turns to* CATHERINE]: You see what he is? [*She turns and grabs* EDDIE's *face in her hands.*] Mmm! You're an angel! God'll bless you. [*He is gratefully smiling.*] You'll see, you'll get a blessing for this!

EDDIE [*laughing*]: I'll settle for my own bed.

BEATRICE: Go, Baby, set the table.

CATHERINE: We didn't tell him about me yet.

BEATRICE: Let him eat first, then we'll tell him. Bring everything in. [*She hurries* CATHERINE *out.*]

EDDIE [*sitting at the table*]: What's all that about? Where's she goin'?

BEATRICE: Noplace. It's very good news, Eddie. I want you to be happy.

EDDIE: What's goin' on?

[CATHERINE *enters with plates, forks.*]

BEATRICE: She's got a job.

[*Pause.* EDDIE *looks at* CATHERINE, *then back to* BEATRICE.]

EDDIE: What job? She's gonna finish school.

CATHERINE: Eddie, you won't believe it –

EDDIE: No – no, you gonna finish school. What kinda job, what do you mean? All of a sudden you –

CATHERINE: Listen a minute, it's wonderful.

EDDIE: It's not wonderful. You'll never get nowheres unless you finish school. You can't take no job. Why didn't you ask me before you take a job?

BEATRICE: She's askin' you now, she didn't take nothin' yet.

CATHERINE: Listen a minute! I came to school this morning and the principal called me out of the class, see? To go to his office.

EDDIE: Yeah?

CATHERINE: So I went in and he says to me he's got my records, y'know? And there's a company wants a girl right away. It ain't exactly a secretary, it's a stenographer first, but pretty soon you get to be secretary. And he says to me that I'm the best student in the whole class –

BEATRICE: You hear that?

EDDIE: Well, why not? Sure she's the best.

CATHERINE: I'm the best student, he says, and if I want, I should take the job and the end of the year he'll let me take the examination and he'll give me the certificate. So I'll save practically a year!

EDDIE [*strangely nervous*]: Where's the job? What company?

CATHERINE: It's a big plumbing company over Nostrand Avenue.

EDDIE: Nostrand Avenue and where?

CATHERINE: It's someplace by the Navy Yard.

BEATRICE: Fifty dollars a week, Eddie.

EDDIE [*to* CATHERINE, *surprised*]: Fifty?

CATHERINE: I swear.

[*Pause.*]

EDDIE: What about all the stuff you wouldn't learn this year, though?

CATHERINE: There's nothin' more to learn, Eddie, I just gotta practise from now on. I know all the symbols and I know the keyboard. I'll just get faster, that's all. And when I'm workin' I'll keep gettin' better and better, you see?

BEATRICE: Work is the best practice anyway.

EDDIE: That ain't what I wanted, though.

CATHERINE: Why! It's a great big company –

EDDIE: I don't like that neighbourhood over there.

CATHERINE: It's a block and half from the subway, he says.

EDDIE: Near the Navy Yard plenty can happen in a block and a half. And a plumbin' company! That's one step over the waterfront. They're practically longshoremen.

BEATRICE: Yeah, but she'll be in the office, Eddie.

EDDIE: I know she'll be in the office, but that ain't what I had in mind.

BEATRICE: Listen, she's gotta go to work sometime.

EDDIE: Listen, B., she'll be with a lotta plumbers? And sailors up and down the street? So what did she go to school for?

CATHERINE: But it's fifty a week, Eddie.

EDDIE: Look, did I ask you for money? I supported you this long, I support you a little more. Please, do me a favour, will ya? I want you to be with different kind of people. I want you to be in a nice office. Maybe a lawyer's office someplace in New York in one of them nice buildings. I mean if you're gonna get outa here then get out; don't go practically in the same kind of neighbourhood.

[*Pause.* CATHERINE *lowers her eyes.*]

BEATRICE: Go, Baby, bring in the supper. [CATHERINE *goes out.*] Think about it a little bit, Eddie. Please. She's crazy to start work. It's not a little shop, it's a big company. Some day she could be a secretary. They picked her out of the whole class. [*He is silent, staring down at the tablecloth fingering the pattern.*] What are you worried about? She could take care of herself. She'll get out of the subway and be in the office in two minutes.

EDDIE [*somehow sickened*]: I know that neighbourhood, B., I don't like it.

BEATRICE: Listen, if nothin' happened to her in this neighbourhood it ain't gonna happen noplace else. [*She turns his face to her.*] Look, you gotta get used to it, she's no baby no more. Tell her to take it. [*He turns his head away.*] You hear me? [*She is angering.*] I don't understand you; she's seventeen years old, you gonna keep her in the house all her life?

EDDIE [*insulted*]: What kinda remark is that?

BEATRICE [*with sympathy but insistent force*]: Well, I don't understand when it ends. First it was gonna be when she graduated high-school, so she graduated high-school. Then it was gonna be when she learned stenographer, so she learned stenographer. So what're we gonna wait for now? I mean it, Eddie, sometimes I don't understand you; they picked her out of the whole class, it's an honour for her.

[CATHERINE *enters with food, which she silently sets on the table. After a moment of watching her face,* EDDIE *breaks into a smile, but it almost seems that tears will form in his eyes.*]

EDDIE: With your hair that way you look like a madonna, you know that? You're the madonna type. [*She doesn't look at him, but continues ladling out food on to the plates.*] You wanna go to work, heh, Madonna?

CATHERINE [*softly*]: Yeah.

EDDIE [*with a sense of her childhood, her babyhood, and the years*]: All right, go to work. [*She looks at him, then rushes and hugs him.*] Hey, hey! Take it easy! [*He holds her face away from him to look at her.*] What're you cryin' about? [*He is affected by her, but smiles his emotion away.*]

CATHERINE [*sitting at her place*]: I just – [*Bursting out*] I'm gonna buy all new dishes with my first pay! [*They laugh warmly.*] I mean it. I'll fix up the whole house! I'll buy a rug!

EDDIE: And then you'll move away.

CATHERINE: No, Eddie!

EDDIE [*grinning*]: Why not? That's life. And you'll come visit on Sundays, then once a month, then Christmas and New Years, finally.

CATHERINE [*grasping his arm to reassure him and to erase the accusation*]: No, please!

EDDIE [*smiling but hurt*]: I only ask you one thing – don't trust nobody. You got a good aunt but she's got too big a heart, you learned bad from her. Believe me.

BEATRICE: Be the way you are, Katie, don't listen to him.

EDDIE [*to BEATRICE – strangely and quickly resentful*]: You lived in a house all your life, what do you know about it? You never worked in your life.

BEATRICE: She likes people. What's wrong with that?

EDDIE: Because most people ain't people. She's goin' to work; plumbers; they'll chew her to pieces if she don't watch out. [*To CATHERINE*] Believe me, Katie, the less you trust, the less you be sorry.

[*EDDIE crosses himself and the women do the same, and they eat.*]

CATHERINE: First thing I'll buy is a rug, heh, B.?

BEATRICE: I don't mind. [*To EDDIE*] I smelled coffee all day today. You unloadin' coffee today?

EDDIE: Yeah, a Brazil ship.

CATHERINE: I smelled it too. It smelled all over the neighbourhood.

EDDIE: That's one time, boy, to be a longshoreman is a pleasure. I could work coffee ships twenty hours a day. You

go down in the hold, y'know? It's like flowers, that smell.
We'll bust a bag tomorrow, I'll bring you some.

BEATRICE: Just be sure there's no spiders in it, will ya? I mean
it. [*She directs this to* CATHERINE, *rolling her eyes upward.*]
I still remember that spider coming out of that bag he brung
home. I nearly died.

EDDIE: You call that a spider? You oughta see what comes
outa the bananas sometimes.

BEATRICE: Don't talk about it!

EDDIE: I seen spiders could stop a Buick.

BEATRICE [*clapping her hands over her ears*]: All right, shut up!

EDDIE [*laughing and taking a watch out of his pocket*]: Well, who
started with spiders?

BEATRICE: All right, I'm sorry, I didn't mean it. Just don't
bring none home again. What time is it?

EDDIE: Quarter nine. [*Puts watch back in his pocket.*]
    [*They continue eating in silence.*]

CATHERINE: He's bringin' them ten o'clock, Tony?

EDDIE: Around, yeah. [*He eats.*]

CATHERINE: Eddie, suppose somebody asks if they're livin'
here. [*He looks at her as though already she had divulged something publicly. Defensively*] I mean if they ask.

EDDIE: Now look, Baby, I can see we're gettin' mixed up
again here.

CATHERINE: No, I just mean . . . people'll see them goin' in
and out.

EDDIE: I don't care who sees them goin' in and out as long as
you don't see them goin' in and out. And this goes for you
too, B. You don't see nothin' and you don't know nothin'.

BEATRICE: What do you mean? I understand.

EDDIE: You don't understand; you still think you can talk
about this to somebody just a little bit. Now lemme say it
once and for all, because you're makin' me nervous again,
both of you. I don't care if somebody comes in the house

and sees them sleepin' on the floor, it never comes out of your mouth who they are or what they're doin' here.

BEATRICE: Yeah, but my mother'll know –

EDDIE: Sure she'll know, but just don't you be the one who told her, that's all. This is the United States government you're playin' with now, this is the Immigration Bureau. If you said it you knew it, if you didn't say it you didn't know it.

CATHERINE: Yeah, but Eddie, suppose somebody –

EDDIE: I don't care what question it is. You – don't – know – nothin'. They got stool pigeons all over this neighbourhood, they're payin' them every week for information, and you don't know who they are. It could be your best friend. You hear? [*To* BEATRICE] Like Vinny Bolzano, remember Vinny?

BEATRICE: Oh, yeah. God forbid.

EDDIE: Tell her about Vinny. [*To* CATHERINE] You think I'm blowin' steam here? [*To* BEATRICE] Go ahead, tell her. [*To* CATHERINE] You was a baby then. There was a family lived next door to her mother, he was about sixteen –

BEATRICE: No, he was no more than fourteen, 'cause I was to his confirmation in Saint Agnes. But the family had an uncle that they were hidin' in the house, and he snitched to the Immigration.

CATHERINE: The kid snitched?

EDDIE: On his own uncle!

CATHERINE: What, was he crazy?

EDDIE: He was crazy after, I tell you that, boy.

BEATRICE: Oh, it was terrible. He had five brothers and the old father. And they grabbed him in the kitchen and pulled him down the stairs – three flights his head was bouncin' like a coconut. And they spit on him in the street, his own father and his brothers. The whole neighbourhood was cryin'.

CATHERINE: Ts! So what happened to him?

BEATRICE: I think he went away. [*To* EDDIE] I never seen him again, did you?

EDDIE [*rises during this, taking out his watch*]: Him? You'll never see him no more, a guy do a thing like that? How's he gonna show his face? [*To* CATHERINE, *as he gets up uneasily*] Just remember, kid, you can quicker get back a million dollars that was stole than a word that you gave away. [*He is standing now, stretching his back.*]

CATHERINE: Okay, I won't say a word to nobody, I swear.

EDDIE: Gonna rain tomorrow. We'll be slidin' all over the decks. Maybe you oughta put something on for them, they be here soon.

BEATRICE: I only got fish, I hate to spoil it if they ate already. I'll wait, it only takes a few minutes; I could broil it.

CATHERINE: What happens, Eddie, when that ship pulls out and they ain't on it, though? Don't the captain say nothin'?

EDDIE [*slicing an apple with his pocket-knife*]: Captain's pieced off, what do you mean?

CATHERINE: Even the captain?

EDDIE: What's the matter, the captain don't have to live? Captain gets a piece, maybe one of the mates, piece for the guy in Italy who fixed the papers for them, Tony here'll get a little bite. ...

BEATRICE: I just hope they get work here, that's all I hope.

EDDIE: Oh, the syndicate'll fix jobs for them; till they pay 'em off they'll get them work every day. It's after the pay-off, then they'll have to scramble like the rest of us.

BEATRICE: Well, it be better than they got there.

EDDIE: Oh sure, well, listen. So you gonna start Monday, heh, Madonna?

CATHERINE [*embarrassed*]: I'm supposed to, yeah.

[EDDIE *is standing facing the two seated women. First* BEATRICE *smiles, then* CATHERINE, *for a powerful emotion is on him, a childish one and a knowing fear, and the tears show in his eyes – and they are shy before the avowal.*]

EDDIE [*sadly smiling, yet somehow proud of her*]: Well ... I hope you have good luck. I wish you the best. You know that, kid.

CATHERINE [*rising, trying to laugh*]: You sound like I'm goin' a million miles!

EDDIE: I know. I guess I just never figured on one thing.

CATHERINE [*smiling*]: What?

EDDIE: That you would ever grow up. [*He utters a soundless laugh at himself, feeling the breast pocket of his shirt.*] I left a cigar in my other coat, I think. [*He starts for the bedroom.*]

CATHERINE: Stay there! I'll get it for you.

[*She hurries out. There is a slight pause, and* EDDIE *turns to* BEATRICE, *who has been avoiding his gaze.*]

EDDIE: What are you mad at me lately?

BEATRICE: Who's mad? [*She gets up, clearing the dishes.*] I'm not mad. [*She picks up the dishes and turns to him.*] You're the one is mad. [*She turns and goes into the kitchen as* CATHERINE *enters from the bedroom with a cigar and a pack of matches.*]

CATHERINE: Here! I'll light it for you! [*She strikes a match and holds it to his cigar. He puffs. Quietly*] Don't worry about me, Eddie, heh?

EDDIE: Don't burn yourself. [*Just in time she blows out the match.*] You better go in help her with the dishes.

CATHERINE [*turns quickly to the table, and, seeing the table cleared, she says, almost guiltily*]: Oh! [*She hurries into the kitchen, and as she exits there*] I'll do the dishes, B.!

[*Alone,* EDDIE *stands looking towards the kitchen for a moment. Then he takes out his watch, glances at it, replaces it in his pocket, sits in the armchair, and stares at the smoke flowing out of his mouth.*

The lights go down, then come up on ALFIERI, *who has moved on to the forestage.*]

ALFIERI: He was as good a man as he had to be in a life that was hard and even. He worked on the piers when there was work, he brought home his pay, and he lived. And towards ten o'clock of that night, after they had eaten, the cousins came.

[*The lights fade on* ALFIERI *and rise on the street.*]

[*Enter* TONY, *escorting* MARCO *and* RODOLPHO, *each with a valise.* TONY *halts, indicates the house. They stand for a moment looking at it.*]

MARCO [– *he is a square-built peasant of thirty-two, suspicious, tender, and quiet-voiced*]: Thank you

TONY: You're on your own now. Just be careful, that's all. Ground floor.

MARCO: Thank you.

TONY [*indicating the house*]: I'll see you on the pier tomorrow. You'll go to work.

[MARCO *nods.* TONY *continues on walking down the street.*]

RODOLPHO: This will be the first house I ever walked into in America! Imagine! She said they were poor!

MARCO: Ssh! Come.

[*They go to door.* MARCO *knocks. The lights rise in the room.* EDDIE *goes and opens the door. Enter* MARCO *and* RODOLPHO, *removing their caps.* BEATRICE *and* CATHERINE *enter from the kitchen. The lights fade in the street.*]

EDDIE: You Marco?

MARCO: Marco.

EDDIE: Come on in! [*He shakes* MARCO'*s hand.*]

BEATRICE: Here, take the bags!

MARCO [*nods, looks to the women, and fixes on* BEATRICE. *Crosses to* BEATRICE.]: Are you my cousin?

[*She nods. He kisses her hand.*]

BEATRICE [*above the table, touching her chest with her hand*]: Beatrice. This is my husband, Eddie. [*All nod.*] Catherine, my sister Nancy's daughter. [*The brothers nod.*]

MARCO [*indicating* RODOLPHO]: My brother. Rodolpho. [RODOLPHO *nods.* MARCO *comes with a certain formal stiffness to* EDDIE.] I want to tell you now Eddie – when you say go, we will go.

EDDIE: Oh, no ... [*Takes* MARCO'S *bag.*]

MARCO: I see it's a small house, but soon, maybe, we can have our own house.

EDDIE: You're welcome, Marco, we got plenty of room here. Katie, give them supper, heh? [*Exits into bedroom with their bags.*]

CATHERINE: Come here, sit down. I'll get you some soup.

MARCO [*as they go to the table*]: We ate on the ship. Thank you. [*To* EDDIE, *calling off to bedroom*] Thank you.

BEATRICE: Get some coffee. We'll all have coffee. Come sit down.

[RODOLPHO *and* MARCO *sit, at the table.*]

CATHERINE [*wondrously*]: How come he's so dark and you're so light, Rodolpho?

RODOLPHO [*ready to laugh*]: I don't know. A thousand years ago, they say, the Danes invaded Sicily.

[BEATRICE *kisses* RODOLPHO. *They laugh as* EDDIE *enters.*]

CATHERINE [*to* BEATRICE]: He's practically blond!

EDDIE: How's the coffee doin'?

CATHERINE [*brought up*]: I'm gettin' it. [*She hurries out to kitchen.*]

EDDIE [*sits on his rocker*]: Yiz have a nice trip?

MARCO: The ocean is always rough. But we are good sailors.

EDDIE: No trouble gettin' here?

MARCO: No. The man brought us. Very nice man.

RODOLPHO [*to* EDDIE]: He says we start to work tomorrow. Is he honest?

EDDIE [*laughing*]: No. But as long as you owe them money, they'll get you plenty of work. [*To* MARCO] Yiz ever work on the piers in Italy?

MARCO: Piers? Ts! – no.

RODOLPHO [*smiling at the smallness of his town*]: In our town there are no piers, only the beach, and little fishing boats.

BEATRICE: So what kinda work did yiz do?

MARCO [*shrugging shyly, even embarrassed*]: Whatever there is, anything.

RODOLPHO: Sometimes they build a house, or if they fix the bridge – Marco is a mason and I bring him the cement. [*He laughs.*] In harvest time we work in the fields ... if there is work. Anything.

EDDIE: Still bad there, heh?

MARCO: Bad, yes.

RODOLPHO [*laughing*]: It's terrible! We stand around all day in the piazza listening to the fountain like birds. Everybody waits only for the train.

BEATRICE: What's on the train?

RODOLPHO: Nothing. But if there are many passengers and you're lucky you make a few lire to push the taxi up the hill.

[*Enter* CATHERINE; *she listens.*]

BEATRICE: You gotta push a taxi?

RODOLPHO [*laughing*]: Oh, sure! It's a feature in our town. The horses in our town are skinnier than goats. So if there are too many passengers we help to push the carriages up to the hotel. [*He laughs.*] In our town the horses are only for show.

CATHERINE: Why don't they have automobile taxis?

RODOLPHO: There is one. We push that too. [*They laugh.*] Everything in our town, you gotta push!

BEATRICE [*to* EDDIE]: How do you like that!

EDDIE [*to* MARCO]: So what're you wanna do, you gonna stay here in this country or you wanna go back?

MARCO [*surprised*]: Go back?

EDDIE: Well, you're married, ain't you?

MARCO: Yes. I have three children.

BEATRICE: Three! I thought only one.

MARCO: Oh, no. I have three now. Four years, five years, six years.

BEATRICE: Ah ... I bet they're cryin' for you already, heh?

MARCO: What can I do? The older one is sick in his chest. My wife – she feeds them from her own mouth. I tell you the truth, if I stay there they will never grow up. They eat the sunshine.

BEATRICE: My God. So how long you want to stay?

MARCO: With your permission, we will stay maybe a –

EDDIE: She don't mean in this house, she means in the country.

MARCO: Oh. Maybe, four, five, six years, I think.

RODOLPHO [*smiling*]: He trusts his wife.

BEATRICE: Yeah, but maybe you'll get enough, you'll be able to go back quicker.

MARCO: I hope. I don't know. [*To* EDDIE] I understand it's not so good here either.

EDDIE: Oh, you guys'll be all right – till you pay them off, anyway. After that, you'll have to scramble, that's all. But you'll make better here than you could there.

RODOLPHO: How much? We hear all kinds of figures. How much can a man make? We work hard, we'll work all day, all night –

[MARCO *raises a hand to hush him.*]

EDDIE [*– he is coming more and more to address* MARCO *only*]: On the average a whole year? Maybe – well, it's hard to say, see. Sometimes we lay off, there's no ships three, four weeks.

MARCO: Three, four weeks! – Ts!

EDDIE: But I think you could probably – thirty, forty a week, over the whole twelve months of the year.

MARCO [*rises, crosses to* EDDIE]: Dollars.

EDDIE: Sure dollars.

[MARCO *puts an arm round* RODOLPHO *and they laugh.*]

MARCO: If we can stay here a few months, Beatrice –

BEATRICE: Listen, you're welcome, Marco –

MARCO: Because I could send them a little more if I stay here.

BEATRICE: As long as you want, we got plenty a room.

MARCO [*his eyes are showing tears*]: My wife – [*To* EDDIE] My wife – I want to send right away maybe twenty dollars –

EDDIE: You could send them something next week already.

MARCO [– *he is near tears*]: Eduardo ... [*He goes to* EDDIE, *offering his hand.*]

EDDIE: Don't thank me. Listen, what the hell, it's no skin off me. [*To* CATHERINE] What happened to the coffee?

CATHERINE: I got it on. [*To* RODOLPHO] You married too? No.

RODOLPHO [*rises*]: Oh, no ...

BEATRICE [*to* CATHERINE]: I told you he –

CATHERINE: I know, I just thought maybe he got married recently.

RODOLPHO: I have no money to get married. I have a nice face, but no money. [*He laughs.*]

CATHERINE [*to* BEATRICE]: He's a real blond!

BEATRICE [*to* RODOLPHO]: You want to stay here too, heh? For good?

RODOLPHO: Me? Yes, for ever! Me, I want to be an American. And then I want to go back to Italy when I am rich, and I will buy a motorcycle. [*He smiles.* MARCO *shakes him affectionately.*]

CATHERINE: A motorcycle!

RODOLPHO: With a motorcycle in Italy you will never starve any more.

BEATRICE: I'll get you coffee. [*She exits to the kitchen.*]

EDDIE: What you do with a motorcycle?

MARCO: He dreams, he dreams.

RODOLPHO [*to* MARCO]: Why? [*To* EDDIE] Messages! The rich people in the hotel always need someone who will carry a message. But quickly, and with a great noise. With a blue motorcycle I would station myself in the courtyard of the hotel, and in a little while I would have messages.

MARCO: When you have no wife you have dreams.

EDDIE: Why can't you just walk, or take a trolley, or sump'm?

[*Enter* BEATRICE *with coffee.*]

RODOLPHO: Oh, no, the machine, the machine is necessary. A man comes into a great hotel and says, I am a messenger. Who is this man? He disappears walking, there is no noise, nothing. Maybe he will never come back, maybe he will never deliver the message. But a man who rides up on a great machine, this man is responsible, this man exists. He will be given messages. [*He helps* BEATRICE *set out the coffee things.*] I am also a singer, though.

EDDIE: You mean a regular – ?

RODOLPHO: Oh, yes. One night last year Andreola got sick. Baritone. And I took his place in the garden of the hotel. Three arias I sang without a mistake! Thousand-lire notes they threw from the tables, money was falling like a storm in the treasury. It was magnificent. We lived six months on that night, eh, Marco?

[MARCO *nods doubtfully.*]

MARCO: Two months.

[EDDIE *laughs.*]

BEATRICE: Can't you get a job in that place?

RODOLPHO: Andreola got better. He's a baritone, very strong.

[BEATRICE *laughs.*]

MARCO [*regretfully, to* BEATRICE]: He sang too loud.

RODOLPHO: Why too loud?

MARCO: Too loud. The guests in that hotel are all Englishmen. They don't like too loud.

RODOLPHO [*to* CATHERINE]: Nobody ever said it was too loud!

MARCO: I say. It was too loud. [*To* BEATRICE] I knew it as soon as he started to sing. Too loud.

RODOLPHO: Then why did they throw so much money?

MARCO: They paid for your courage. The English like courage. But once is enough.

RODOLPHO [*to all but* MARCO]: I never heard anybody say it was too loud.

CATHERINE: Did you ever hear of jazz?

RODOLPHO: Oh, sure! I *sing* jazz.

CATHERINE [*rises*]: You could sing jazz?

RODOLPHO: Oh, I sing Napolidan, jazz, *bel canto* – I sing *Paper Doll*, you like *Paper Doll*?

CATHERINE: Oh, sure. I'm crazy for *Paper Doll*. Go ahead, sing it.

RODOLPHO [*takes his stance after getting a nod of permission from* MARCO, *and with a high tenor voice begins singing*]:
    I'll tell you boys it's tough to be alone,
    And it's tough to love a doll that's not your own.
    I'm through with all of them,
    I'll never fall again,
    Hey, boy, what you gonna do?
    I'm gonna buy a paper doll that I can call my own,
    A doll that other fellows cannot steal.
    [EDDIE *rises and moves upstage.*]
    And then those flirty, flirty guys
    With their flirty, flirty eyes
    Will have to flirt with dollies that are real –

EDDIE: Hey, kid – hey, wait a minute –

CATHERINE [*enthralled*]: Leave him finish, it's beautiful! [*To* BEATRICE] He's terrific! It's terrific, Rodolpho.

EDDIE: Look, kid; you don't want to be picked up, do ya?

MARCO: No – no! [*He rises.*]

EDDIE [*indicating the rest of the building*]: Because we never had no singers here ... and all of a sudden there's a singer in the house, y'know what I mean?

MARCO: Yes, yes. You'll be quiet, Rodolpho.

EDDIE [– *he is flushed*]: They got guys all over the place, Marco. I mean.

MARCO: Yes. He'll be quiet. [*To* RODOLPHO] You'll be quiet.

> [RODOLPHO *nods.*
>
> EDDIE *has risen, with iron control, even a smile. He moves to* CATHERINE.]

EDDIE: What's the high heels for, Garbo?

CATHERINE: I figured for tonight –

EDDIE: Do me a favour, will you? Go ahead.

> [*Embarrassed now, angered,* CATHERINE *goes out into the bedroom.* BEATRICE *watches her go and gets up; in passing, she gives* EDDIE *a cold look, restrained only by the strangers, and goes to the table to pour coffee.*]

EDDIE [*striving to laugh, and to* MARCO, *but directed as much to* BEATRICE]: All actresses they want to be around here.

RODOLPHO [*happy about it*]: In Italy too! All the girls.

> [CATHERINE *emerges from the bedroom in low-heel shoes, comes to the table.* RODOLPHO *is lifting a cup.*]

EDDIE [– *he is sizing up* RODOLPHO, *and there is a concealed suspicion*]: Yeah, heh?

RODOLPHO: Yes! [*Laughs, indicating* CATHERINE] Especially when they are so beautiful!

CATHERINE: You like sugar?

RODOLPHO: Sugar? Yes! I like sugar very much!

> [EDDIE *is downstage, watching as she pours a spoonful of sugar into his cup, his face puffed with trouble, and the room dies.*
>
> *Lights rise on* ALFIERI.]

ALFIERI: Who can ever know what will be discovered? Eddie

Carbone had never expected to have a destiny. A man works, raises his family, goes bowling, eats, gets old, and then he dies. Now, as the weeks passed, there was a future, there was a trouble that would not go away.

[*The lights fade on* ALFIERI, *then rise on* EDDIE *standing at the doorway of the house.* BEATRICE *enters on the street. She sees* EDDIE, *smiles at him. He looks away.*

She starts to enter the house when EDDIE *speaks.*]

EDDIE: It's after eight.

BEATRICE: Well, it's a long show at the Paramount.

EDDIE: They must've seen every picture in Brooklyn by now. He's supposed to stay in the house when he ain't working. He ain't supposed to go advertising himself.

BEATRICE: Well, that's his trouble, what do you care? If they pick him up they pick him up, that's all. Come in the house.

EDDIE: What happened to the stenography? I don't see her practise no more.

BEATRICE: She'll get back to it. She's excited, Eddie.

EDDIE: She tell you anything?

BEATRICE [*comes to him, now the subject is opened*]: What's the matter with you? He's a nice kid, what do you want from him?

EDDIE: That's a nice kid? He gives me the heeby-jeebies.

BEATRICE [*smiling*]: Ah, go on, you're just jealous.

EDDIE: Of *him*? Boy, you don't think much of me.

BEATRICE: I don't understand you. What's so terrible about him?

EDDIE: You mean it's all right with you? That's gonna be her husband?

BEATRICE: Why? He's a nice fella, hard workin', he's a good-lookin' fella.

EDDIE: He sings on the ships, didja know that?

BEATRICE: What do you mean, he sings?

EDDIE: Just what I said, he sings. Right on the deck, all of a sudden, a whole song comes out of his mouth – with motions. You know what they're callin' him now? Paper Doll they're callin' him, Canary. He's like a weird. He comes out on the pier, one-two-three, it's a regular free show.

BEATRICE: Well, he's a kid; he don't know how to behave himself yet.

EDDIE: And with that wacky hair; he's like a chorus girl or sump'm.

BEATRICE: So he's blond, so –

EDDIE: I just hope that's his regular hair, that's all I hope.

BEATRICE: You crazy or sump'm? [*She tries to turn him to her.*]

EDDIE [– *he keeps his head turned away*]: What's so crazy? I don't like his whole way.

BEATRICE: Listen, you never seen a blond guy in your life? What about Whitey Balso?

EDDIE [*turning to her victoriously*]: Sure, but Whitey don't sing; he don't do like that on the ships.

BEATRICE: Well, maybe that's the way they do in Italy.

EDDIE: Then why don't his brother sing? Marco goes around like a man; nobody kids Marco. [*He moves from her, halts. She realizes there is a campaign solidified in him.*] I tell you the truth I'm surprised I have to tell you all this. I mean I'm surprised, B.

BEATRICE [– *she goes to him with purpose now*]: Listen, you ain't gonna start nothin' here.

EDDIE: I ain't startin' nothin', but I ain't gonna stand around lookin' at that. For that character I didn't bring her up. I swear, B., I'm surprised at you; I sit there waitin' for you to wake up but everything is great with you.

BEATRICE: No, everything ain't great with me.

EDDIE: No?

BEATRICE: No. But I got other worries.

EDDIE: Yeah. [*He is already weakening.*]

BEATRICE: Yeah, you want me to tell you?

EDDIE [*in retreat*]: Why? What worries you got?

BEATRICE: When am I gonna be a wife again, Eddie?

EDDIE: I ain't been feelin' good. They bother me since they came.

BEATRICE: It's almost three months you don't feel good; they're only here a couple of weeks. It's three months, Eddie.

EDDIE: I don't know, B. I don't want to talk about it.

BEATRICE: What's the matter, Eddie, you don't like me, heh?

EDDIE: What do you mean, I don't like you? I said I don't feel good, that's all.

BEATRICE: Well, tell me, am I doing something wrong? Talk to me.

EDDIE [– *Pause. He can't speak, then*]: I can't. I can't talk about it.

BEATRICE: Well tell me what –

EDDIE: I got nothin' to say about it!

[*She stands for a moment; he is looking off; she turns to go into the house.*]

EDDIE: I'll be all right, B.; just lay off me, will ya? I'm worried about her.

BEATRICE: The girl is gonna be eighteen years old, it's time already.

EDDIE: B., he's taking her for a ride!

BEATRICE: All right, that's her ride. What're you gonna stand over her till she's forty? Eddie, I want you to cut it out now, you hear me? I don't like it! Now come in the house.

EDDIE: I want to take a walk, I'll be in right away.

BEATRICE: They ain't goin' to come any quicker if you stand in the street. It ain't nice, Eddie.

EDDIE: I'll be in right away. Go ahead.

[*He walks off. She goes into the house.* EDDIE *glances up the street, sees* LOUIS *and* MIKE *coming, and sits on an iron railing.* LOUIS *and* MIKE *enter.*]

LOUIS: Wanna go bowlin' tonight?

EDDIE: I'm too tired. Goin' to sleep.

LOUIS: How's your two submarines?

EDDIE: They're okay.

LOUIS: I see they're gettin' work allatime.

EDDIE: Oh yeah, they're doin' all right.

MIKE: That's what we oughta do. We oughta leave the country and come in under the water. Then we get work.

EDDIE: You ain't kiddin'.

LOUIS: Well, what the hell. Y'know?

EDDIE: Sure.

LOUIS [*– sits on railing beside* EDDIE]: Believe me, Eddie, you got a lotta credit comin' to you.

EDDIE: Aah, they don't bother me, don't cost me nutt'n.

MIKE: That older one, boy, he's a regular bull. I seen him the other day liftin' coffee bags over the Matson Line. They leave him alone he woulda load the whole ship by himself.

EDDIE: Yeah, he's a strong guy, that guy. Their father was a regular giant, supposed to be.

LOUIS: Yeah, you could see. He's a regular slave.

MIKE [*grinning*]: That blond one, though – [EDDIE *looks at him.*] He's got a sense of humour. [LOUIS *snickers.*]

EDDIE [*searchingly*]: Yeah. He's funny –

MIKE [*starting to laugh*]: Well he ain't exackly funny, but he's always like makin' remarks like, y'know? He comes around, everybody's laughin'. [LOUIS *laughs.*]

EDDIE [*uncomfortably grinning*]: Yeah, well … he's got a sense of humour.

MIKE [*laughing*]: Yeah, I mean, he's always makin' like remarks, like, y'know?

EDDIE: Yeah, I know. But he's a kid yet, y'know? He – he's just a kid, that's all.

MIKE [*getting hysterical with* LOUIS]: I know. You take one look at him – everybody's happy. [LOUIS *laughs.*] I worked one day with him last week over the Moore-MacCormack Line, I'm tellin' you they was all hysterical. [LOUIS *and he explode in laughter.*]

EDDIE: Why? What'd he do?

MIKE: I don't know ... he was just humorous. You never can remember what he says, y'know? But it's the way he says it. I mean he gives you a look sometimes and you start laughin'!

EDDIE: Yeah. [*Troubled*] He's got a sense of humour.

MIKE [*gasping*]: Yeah.

LOUIS [*rising*]: Well, we see ya, Eddie.

EDDIE: Take it easy.

LOUIS: Yeah. See ya.

MIKE: If you wanna come bowlin' later we're goin' Flatbush Avenue.

[*Laughing, they move to exit, meeting* RODOLPHO *and* CATHERINE *entering on the street. Their laughter rises as they see* RODOLPHO, *who does not understand but joins in.* EDDIE *moves to enter the house as* LOUIS *and* MIKE *exit.* CATHERINE *stops him at the door.*]

CATHERINE: Hey, Eddie – what a picture we saw! Did we laugh!

EDDIE [– *he can't help smiling at sight of her*]: Where'd you go?

CATHERINE: Paramount. It was with those two guys, y'know? That –

EDDIE: Brooklyn Paramount?

CATHERINE [*with an edge of anger, embarrassed before* RODOLPHO]: Sure, the Brooklyn Paramount. I told you we wasn't goin' to New York.

EDDIE [*retreating before the threat of her anger*]: All right, I only asked you. [*To* RODOLPHO] I just don't want her hangin' around Times Square, see? It's full of tramps over there.

RODOLPHO: I would like to go to Broadway once, Eddie. I would like to walk with her once where the theatres are and the opera. Since I was a boy I see pictures of those lights.

EDDIE [*his little patience waning*]: I want to talk to her a minute, Rodolpho. Go inside, will you?

RODOLPHO: Eddie, we only walk together in the streets. She teaches me.

CATHERINE: You know what he can't get over? That there's no fountains in Brooklyn!

EDDIE [*smiling unwillingly*]: Fountains? [RODOLPHO *smiles at his own naïveté.*]

CATHERINE: In Italy he says, every town's got fountains, and they meet there. And you know what? They got oranges on the trees where he comes from, and lemons. Imagine – on the trees? I mean it's interesting. But he's crazy for New York.

RODOLPHO [*attempting familiarity*]: Eddie, why can't we go once to Broadway – ?

EDDIE: Look, I gotta tell her something –

RODOLPHO: Maybe you can come too. I want to see all those lights. [*He sees no response in* EDDIE'*s face. He glances at* CATHERINE.] I'll walk by the river before I go to sleep. [*He walks off down the street.*]

CATHERINE: Why don't you talk to him, Eddie? He blesses you, and you don't talk to him hardly.

EDDIE [*enveloping her with his eyes*]: I bless you and you don't talk to me. [*He tries to smile.*]

CATHERINE: *I* don't talk to you? [*She hits his arm.*] What do you mean?

EDDIE: I don't see you no more. I come home you're runnin' around someplace –

CATHERINE: Well, he wants to see everything, that's all, so we go. ... You mad at me?

EDDIE: No. [*He moves from her, smiling sadly.*] It's just I used to come home, you was always there. Now, I turn around, you're a big girl. I don't know how to talk to you.

CATHERINE: Why?

EDDIE: I don't know, you're runnin', you're runnin', Katie. I don't think you listening any more to me.

CATHERINE [going to him]: Ah, Eddie, sure I am. What's the matter? You don't like him?

[Slight pause.]

EDDIE [turns to her]: You like him, Katie?

CATHERINE [with a blush but holding her ground]: Yeah. I like him.

EDDIE [– his smile goes]: You like him.

CATHERINE [looking down]: Yeah. [Now she looks at him for the consequences, smiling but tense. He looks at her like a lost boy.] What're you got against him? I don't understand. He only blesses you.

EDDIE [turns away]: He don't bless me, Katie.

CATHERINE: He does! You're like a father to him!

EDDIE [turns to her]: Katie.

CATHERINE: What, Eddie?

EDDIE: You gonna marry him?

CATHERINE: I don't know. We just been ... goin' around, that's all. [Turns to him.] What're you got against him, Eddie? Please, tell me. What?

EDDIE: He don't respect you.

CATHERINE: Why?

EDDIE: Katie ... if you wasn't an orphan, wouldn't he ask your father's permission before he run around with you like this?

CATHERINE: Oh, well, he didn't think you'd mind.

EDDIE: He knows I mind, but it don't bother him if I mind, don't you see that?

CATHERINE: No, Eddie, he's got all kinds of respect for me. And you too! We walk across the street he takes my arm –

he almost bows to me! You got him all wrong, Eddie; I
mean it, you –

EDDIE: Katie, he's only bowin' to his passport.

CATHERINE: His passport!

EDDIE: That's right. He marries you he's got the right to be
an American citizen. That's what's goin' on here. [*She is
puzzled and surprised.*] You understand what I'm tellin' you?
The guy is lookin' for his break, that's all he's lookin' for.

CATHERINE [*pained*]: Oh, no, Eddie, I don't think so.

EDDIE: You don't think so! Katie, you're gonna make me cry
here. Is that a workin' man? What does he do with his first
money? A snappy new jacket he buys, records, a pointy
pair new shoes and his brother's kids are starvin' over there
with tuberculosis? That's a hit-and-run guy, baby; he's got
bright lights in his head, Broadway. Them guys don't think
of nobody but theirself! You marry him and the next time
you see him it'll be for divorce!

CATHERINE [*steps towards him*]: Eddie, he never said a word
about his papers or –

EDDIE: You mean he's supposed to tell you that?

CATHERINE: I don't think he's even thinking about it.

EDDIE: What's better for him to think about! He could be
picked up any day here and he's back pushin' taxis up the
hill!

CATHERINE: No, I don't believe it.

EDDIE: Katie, don't break my heart, listen to me.

CATHERINE: I don't want to hear it.

EDDIE: Katie, listen ...

CATHERINE: He loves me!

EDDIE [*with deep alarm*]: Don't say that, for God's sake! This
is the oldest racket in the country –

CATHERINE [*desperately, as though he had made his imprint*]: I
don't believe it! [*She rushes to the house.*]

EDDIE [*following her*]: They been pullin' this since the

Immigration Law was put in! They grab a green kid that don't know nothin' and they –

CATHERINE [*sobbing*]: I don't believe it and I wish to hell you'd stop it!

EDDIE: Katie!

[*They enter the apartment. The lights in the living-room have risen and* BEATRICE *is there. She looks past the sobbing* CATHERINE *at* EDDIE, *who in the presence of his wife, makes an awkward gesture of eroded command, indicating* CATHERINE.]

EDDIE: Why don't you straighten her out?

BEATRICE [*inwardly angered at his flowing emotion, which in itself alarms her*]: When are you going to leave her alone?

EDDIE: B., the guy is no good!

BEATRICE [*suddenly, with open fright and fury*]: You going to leave her alone? Or you gonna drive me crazy? [*He turns, striving to retain his dignity, but nevertheless in guilt walks out of the house, into the street and away.* CATHERINE *starts into a bedroom.*] Listen, Catherine. [CATHERINE *halts, turns to her sheepishly.*] What are you going to do with yourself?

CATHERINE: I don't know.

BEATRICE: Don't tell me you don't know; you're not a baby any more, what are you going to do with yourself?

CATHERINE: He won't listen to me.

BEATRICE: I don't understand this. He's not your father, Catherine. I don't understand what's going on here.

CATHERINE [*as one who herself is trying to rationalize a buried impulse*]: What am I going to do, just kick him in the face with it?

BEATRICE: Look, honey, you wanna get married, or don't you wanna get married? What are you worried about, Katie?

CATHERINE [*quietly trembling*]: I don't know B. It just seems wrong if he's against it so much.

BEATRICE [*never losing her aroused alarm*]: Sit down, honey, I want to tell you something. Here, sit down. Was there ever any fella he liked for you? There wasn't, was there?

CATHERINE: But he says Rodolpho's just after his papers.

BEATRICE: Look, he'll say anything. What does he care what he says? If it was a prince came here for you it would be no different. You know that, don't you?

CATHERINE: Yeah, I guess.

BEATRICE: So what does that mean?

CATHERINE [*slowly turns her head to* BEATRICE]: What?

BEATRICE: It means you gotta be your own self more. You still think you're a little girl, honey. But nobody else can make up your mind for you any more, you understand? You gotta give him to understand that he can't give you orders no more.

CATHERINE: Yeah, but how am I going to do that? He thinks I'm a baby.

BEATRICE: Because *you* think you're a baby. I told you fifty times already, you can't act the way you act. You still walk around in front of him in your slip –

CATHERINE: Well I forgot.

BEATRICE: Well you can't do it. Or like you sit on the edge of the bathtub talkin' to him when he's shavin' in his underwear.

CATHERINE: When'd I do that?

BEATRICE: I seen you in there this morning.

CATHERINE: Oh ... well, I wanted to tell him something and I –

BEATRICE: I know, honey. But if you act like a baby and he be treatin' you like a baby. Like when he comes home sometimes you throw youself at him like when you was twelve years old.

CATHERINE: Well I like to see him and I'm happy so I –

BEATRICE: Look, I'm not tellin' you what to do honey, but –

CATHERINE: No, you could tell me, B.! Gee, I'm all mixed up. See, I – He looks so sad now and it hurts me.

BEATRICE: Well look, Katie, if it's goin' to hurt you so much you're gonna end up an old maid here.

CATHERINE: No!

BEATRICE: I'm tellin' you, I'm not makin' a joke. I tried to tell you a couple of times in the last year or so. That's why I was so happy you were going to go out and get work, you wouldn't be here so much, you'd be a little more independent. I mean it. It's wonderful for a whole family to love each other, but you're a grown woman and you're in the same house with a grown man. So you'll act different now, heh?

CATHERINE: Yeah, I will. I'll remember.

BEATRICE: Because it ain't only up to him, Katie, you understand? I told him the same thing already.

CATHERINE [quickly]: What?

BEATRICE: That he should let you go. But, you see, if only I tell him, he thinks I'm just bawlin' him out, or maybe I'm jealous or somethin', you know?

CATHERINE [astonished]: He said you was jealous?

BEATRICE: No, I'm just sayin' maybe that's what he thinks. [She reaches over to CATHERINE's hand; with a strained smile] You think I'm jealous of you, honey?

CATHERINE: No! It's the first I thought of it.

BEATRICE [with a quiet sad laugh]: Well you should have thought of it before ... but I'm not. We'll be all right. Just give him to understand; you don't have to fight, you're just – You're a woman, that's all, and you got a nice boy, and now the time came when you said good-bye. All right?

CATHERINE [strangely moved at the prospect]: All right. . . . If I can.

BEATRICE: Honey ... you gotta.

[CATHERINE, sensing now an imperious demand, turns with

some fear, with a discovery, to BEATRICE. *She is at the edge of tears, as though a familiar world had shattered.*]

CATHERINE: Okay.

[*Lights out on them and up on* ALFIERI, *seated behind his desk.*]

ALFIERI: It was at this time that he first came to me. I had represented his father in an accident case some years before, and I was acquainted with the family in a casual way. I remember him now as he walked through my doorway –

[*Enter* EDDIE *down right ramp.*]

His eyes were like tunnels; my first thought was that he had committed a crime,

[EDDIE *sits beside the desk, cap in hand, looking out.*]

but soon I saw it was only a passion that had moved into his body, like a stranger. [ALFIERI *pauses, looks down at his desk, then to* EDDIE *as though he were continuing a conversation with him.*] I don't quite understand what I can do for you. Is there a question of law somewhere?

EDDIE: That's what I want to ask you.

ALFIERI: Because there's nothing illegal about a girl falling in love with an immigrant.

EDDIE: Yeah, but what about it if the only reason for it is to get his papers?

ALFIERI: First of all you don't know that.

EDDIE: I see it in his eyes; he's laughin' at her and he's laughin' at me.

ALFIERI: Eddie, I'm a lawyer. I can only deal in what's provable. You understand that, don't you? Can you prove that?

EDDIE: *I know what's in his mind, Mr Alfieri!*

ALFIERI: Eddie, even if you could prove that –

EDDIE: Listen ... will you listen to me a minute? My father always said you was a smart man. I want you to listen to me.

ALFIERI: I'm only a lawyer, Eddie.

EDDIE: Will you listen a minute? I'm talkin' about the law. Lemme just bring out what I mean. A man, which he comes into the country illegal, don't it stand to reason he's gonna take every penny and put it in the sock? Because they don't know from one day to another, right?

ALFIERI: All right.

EDDIE: He's spendin'. Records he buys now. Shoes. Jackets. Y'understand me? This guy ain't worried. This guy is *here*. So it must be that he's got it all laid out in his mind already – he's stayin'. Right?

ALFIERI: Well? What about it?

EDDIE: All right. [*He glances at* ALFIERI, *then down to the floor.*] I'm talking to you confidential, ain't I?

ALFIERI: Certainly.

EDDIE: I mean it don't go no place but here. Because I don't like to say this about anybody. Even my wife I didn't exactly say this.

ALFIERI: What is it?

EDDIE [*takes a breath and glances briefly over each shoulder*]: The guy ain't right, Mr Alfieri.

ALFIERI: What do you mean?

EDDIE: I mean he ain't right.

ALFIERI: I don't get you.

EDDIE [*shifts to another position in the chair*]: Dja ever get a look at him?

ALFIERI: Not that I know of, no.

EDDIE: He's a blond guy. Like ... platinum. You know what I mean?

ALFIERI: No.

EDDIE: I mean if you close the paper fast – you could blow him over.

ALFIERI: Well that doesn't mean –

EDDIE: Wait a minute, I'm tellin' you sump'm. He sings, see. Which is – I mean it's all right, but sometimes he hits a note, see. I turn around. I mean – high. You know what I mean?

ALFIERI: Well, that's a tenor.

EDDIE: I know a tenor, Mr Alfieri. This ain't no tenor. I mean if you came in the house and you didn't know who was singin', you wouldn't be lookin' for him you be lookin' for her.

ALFIERI: Yes, but that's not –

EDDIE: I'm tellin' you sump'm, wait a minute. Please, Mr Alfieri. I'm tryin' to bring out my thoughts here. Couple of nights ago my niece brings out a dress which it's too small for her, because she shot up like a light this last year. He takes the dress, lays it on the table, he cuts it up; one-two-three, he makes a new dress. I mean he looked so sweet there, like an angel – you could kiss him he was so sweet.

ALFIERI: Now look, Eddie –

EDDIE: Mr Alfieri, they're laughin' at him on the piers. I'm ashamed. Paper Doll they call him. Blondie now. His brother thinks it's because he's got a sense of humour, see – which he's got – but that ain't what they're laughin'. Which they're not goin' to come out with it because they know he's my relative, which they have to see me if they make a crack, y'know? But I know what they're laughin' at, and when I think of that guy layin' his hands on her I could – I mean it's eatin' me out, Mr Alfieri, because I struggled for that girl. And now he comes in my house and –

ALFIERI: Eddie, look – I have my own children. I understand you. But the law is very specific. The law does not …

EDDIE [*with a fuller flow of indignation*]: You mean to tell me that there's no law that a guy which he ain't right can go to work and marry a girl and – ?

ALFIERI: You have no recourse in the law. Eddie.

EDDIE: Yeah, but if he ain't right, Mr Alfieri, you mean to tell me –

ALFIERI: There is nothing you can do, Eddie, believe me.

EDDIE: Nothin'.

ALFIERI: Nothing at all. There's only one legal question here.

EDDIE: What?

ALFIERI: The manner in which they entered the country. But I don't think you want to do anything about that, do you?

EDDIE: You mean – ?

ALFIERI: Well, they entered illegally.

EDDIE: Oh, Jesus, no, I wouldn't do nothin' about that, I mean –

ALFIERI: All right, then, let me talk now, eh?

EDDIE: Mr Alfieri, I can't believe what you tell me. I mean there must be some kinda law which –

ALFIERI: Eddie, I want you to listen to me. [Pause.] You know, sometimes God mixes up the people. We all love somebody, the wife, the kids – every man's got somebody that he loves, heh? But sometimes ... there's too much. You know? There's too much, and it goes where it mustn't. A man works hard, he brings up a child, sometimes it's a niece, sometimes even a daughter, and he never realizes it, but through the years – there is too much love for the daughter, there is too much love for the niece. Do you understand what I'm saying to you?

EDDIE [sardonically]: What do you mean, I shouldn't look out for her good?

ALFIERI: Yes, but those things have to end, Eddie, that's all. The child has to grow up and go away, and the man has to learn to forget. Because after all, Eddie – what other way can it end? [Pause.] Let her go. That's my advice. You did your job, now it's her life; wish her luck, and let her go. [Pause.] Will you do that? Because there's no law, Eddie; make up your mind to it; the law is not interested in this.

EDDIE: You mean to tell me, even if he's a punk? If he's –

ALFIERI: There's nothing you can do.

[EDDIE *stands.*]

EDDIE: Well, all right, thanks. Thanks very much.

ALFIERI: What are you going to do?

EDDIE [*with a helpless but ironic gesture*]: What can I do? I'm a patsy, what can a patsy do? I worked like a dog twenty years so a punk could have her, so that's what I done. I mean, in the worst times, in the worst, when there wasn't a ship comin' in the harbour, I didn't stand around lookin' for relief – I hustled. When there was empty piers in Brooklyn I went to Hoboken, Staten Island, the West Side, Jersey, all over – because I made a promise. I took out of my own mouth to give to her. I took out of my wife's mouth. I walked hungry plenty days in this city! [*It begins to break through.*] And now I gotta sit in my own house and look at a son-of-a-bitch punk like that – which he came out of nowhere! I give him my house to sleep! I take the blankets off my bed for him, and he takes and puts his dirty filthy hands on her like a goddam thief!

ALFIERI [*rising*]: But, Eddie, she's a woman now.

EDDIE: He's stealing from me!

ALFIERI: She wants to get married, Eddie. She can't marrv you, can she?

EDDIE [*furiously*]: What're you talkin' about, marry me! I don't know what the hell you're talkin' about!

[*Pause.*]

ALFIERI: I gave you my advice, Eddie. That's it.

[EDDIE *gathers himself. A pause.*]

EDDIE: Well, thanks. Thanks very much. It just – it's breakin' my heart, y'know. I –

ALFIERI: I understand. Put it out of your mind. Can you do that?

EDDIE: I'm – [*He feels the threat of sobs, and with a helpless wave*] I'll see you around. [*He goes out up the right ramp.*]

ALFIERI [*sits on desk*]: There are times when you want to

V.F.B.–3

spread an alarm, but nothing has happened. I knew, I knew then and there – I could have finished the whole story that afternoon. It wasn't as though there was a mystery to unravel. I could see every step coming, step after step, like a dark figure walking down a hall towards a certain door. I knew where he was heading for, I knew where he was going to end. And I sat here many afternoons asking myself why, being an intelligent man, I was so powerless to stop it. I even went to a certain old lady in the neighbourhood, a very wise old woman, and I told her, and she only nodded, and said, 'Pray for him ...' And so I – waited here.

[*As lights go out on* ALFIERI, *they rise in the apartment where all are finishing dinner.* BEATRICE *and* CATHERINE *are clearing the table.*]

CATHERINE: You know where they went?

BEATRICE: Where?

CATHERINE: They went to Africa once. On a fishing boat. [EDDIE *glances at her.*] It's true, Eddie.

[BEATRICE *exits into the kitchen with dishes.*]

EDDIE: I didn't say nothin'. [*He goes to his rocker, picks up a newspaper.*]

CATHERINE: And I was never even in Staten Island.

EDDIE [*sitting with the paper*]: You didn't miss nothin'. [*Pause.* CATHERINE *takes dishes out.*] How long that take you, Marco – to get to Africa?

MARCO [*rising*]: Oh ... two days. We go all over.

RODOLPHO [*rising*]: Once we went to Yugoslavia.

EDDIE [*to* MARCO]: They pay all right on them boats?

[BEATRICE *enters. She and* RODOLPHO *stack the remaining dishes.*]

MARCO: If they catch fish they pay all right. [*Sits on a stool.*]

RODOLPHO: They're family boats, though. And nobody in our family owned one. So we only worked when one of the families was sick.

BEATRICE: Y'know, Marco, what I don't understand – there's an ocean full of fish and yiz are all starvin'.

EDDIE: They gotta have boats, nets, you need money.

[CATHERINE enters.]

BEATRICE: Yeah, but couldn't they like fish from the beach? You see them down Coney Island –

MARCO: Sardines.

EDDIE: Sure. [Laughing] How you gonna catch sardines on a hook?

BEATRICE: Oh, I didn't know they're sardines. [To CATHERINE] They're sardines!

CATHERINE: Yeah, they follow them all over the ocean, Africa, Yugoslavia ... [She sits and begins to look through a movie magazine. RODOLPHO joins her.]

BEATRICE [to EDDIE]: It's funny, y'know. You never think of it, that sardines are swimming in the ocean! [She exits to kitchen with dishes.]

CATHERINE: I know. It's like oranges and lemons on a tree. [To EDDIE] I mean you ever think of oranges and lemons on a tree?

EDDIE: Yeah, I know. It's funny. [To MARCO] I heard that they paint the oranges to make them look orange.

[BEATRICE enters.]

MARCO [– He has been reading a letter]: Paint?

EDDIE: Yeah, I heard that they grow like green.

MARCO: No, in Italy the oranges are orange.

RODOLPHO: Lemons are green.

EDDIE [resenting his instruction]: I know lemons are green, for Christ's sake, you see them in the store they're green sometimes. I said oranges they paint, I didn't say nothin' about lemons.

BEATRICE [sitting; diverting their attention]: Your wife is gettin' the money all right, Marco?

MARCO: Oh, yes. She bought medicine for my boy.

BEATRICE: That's wonderful. You feel better, heh?

MARCO: Oh, yes! But I'm lonesome.

BEATRICE: I just hope you ain't gonna do like some of them around here. They're here twenty-five years, some men, and they didn't get enough together to go back twice.

MARCO: Oh, I know. We have many families in our town, the children never saw the father. But I will go home. Three, four years, I think.

BEATRICE: Maybe you should keep more here. Because maybe she thinks it comes so easy you'll never get ahead of yourself.

MARCO: Oh, no, she saves. I send everything. My wife is very lonesome. [He smiles shyly.]

BEATRICE: She must be nice. She pretty? I bet, heh?

MARCO [blushing]: No, but she understand everything.

RODOLPHO: Oh, he's got a clever wife!

EDDIE: I betcha there's plenty surprises sometimes when those guys get back there, heh?

MARCO: Surprises?

EDDIE [laughing]: I mean, you know – they count the kids and there's a couple extra than when they left?

MARCO: No – no ... The women wait, Eddie. Most. Most. Very few surprises.

RODOLPHO: It's more strict in our town. [EDDIE looks at him now.] It's not so free.

EDDIE [rises, paces up and down]: It ain't so free here either, Rodolpho, like you think. I seen greenhorns sometimes get in trouble that way – they think just because a girl don't go around with a shawl over her head that she ain't strict, y'know? Girl don't have to wear black dress to be strict. Know what I mean?

RODOLPHO: Well, I always have respect –

EDDIE: I know, but in your town you wouldn't just drag off some girl without permission, I mean. [He turns.] You know what I mean, Marco? It ain't that much different here.

MARCO [*cautiously*]: Yes.

BEATRICE: Well, he didn't exactly drag her off though, Eddie.

EDDIE: I know, but I seen some of them get the wrong idea sometimes. [*To* RODOLPHO] I mean it might be a little more free here but it's just as strict.

RODOLPHO: I have respect for her, Eddie. I do anything wrong?

EDDIE: Look, kid, I ain't her father, I'm only her uncle –

BEATRICE: Well then, be an uncle then. [EDDIE *looks at her, aware of her criticizing force.*] I mean

MARCO: No, Beatrice, if he does wrong you must tell him. [*To* EDDIE] What does he do wrong?

EDDIE: Well, Marco, till he came here she was never out on the street twelve o'clock at night

MARCO [*to* RODOLPHO]: You come home early now.

BEATRICE [*to* CATHERINE]: Well, you said the movie ended late, didn't you?

CATHERINE: Yeah.

BEATRICE: Well, tell him, honey. [*To* EDDIE] The movie ended late.

EDDIE: Look, B., I'm just sayin' – he thinks she always stayed out like that.

MARCO: You come home early now, Rodolpho.

RODOLPHO [*embarrassed*]: All right, sure. But I can't stay in the house all the time, Eddie.

EDDIE: Look, kid, I'm not only talkin' about her. The more you run around like that the more chance you're takin'. [*To* BEATRICE] I mean suppose he gets hit by a car or something. [*To* MARCO] Where's his papers, who is he? Know what I mean?

BEATRICE: Yeah, but who is he in the daytime, though? It's the same chance in the daytime.

EDDIE [*holding back a voice full of anger*]: Yeah, but he don't
have to go lookin' for it, Beatrice. If he's here to work,
then he should work; if he's here for a good time then he
could fool around! [*To* MARCO] But I understood, Marco,
that you was both comin' to make a livin' for your family.
You understand me, don't you, Marco? [*He goes to his
rocker.*]

MARCO: I beg your pardon, Eddie.

EDDIE: I mean, that's what I understood in the first place, see.

MARCO: Yes. That's why we came.

EDDIE [*sits on his rocker*]: Well, that's all I'm askin'.

    [EDDIE *reads his paper. There is a pause, an awkwardness.
Now* CATHERINE *gets up and puts a record on the phonograph* – Paper Doll.]

CATHERINE [*flushed with revolt*]: You wanna dance, Rodolpho? [EDDIE *freezes.*]

RODOLPHO [*in deference to* EDDIE]: No, I – I'm tired.

BEATRICE: Go ahead, dance, Rodolpho.

CATHERINE: Ah, come on. They got a beautiful quartet, these
guys. Come.

    [*She has taken his hand and he stiffly rises, feeling* EDDIE'*s
eyes on his back, and they dance.*]

EDDIE [*to* CATHERINE]: What's that, a new record?

CATHERINE: It's the same one. We bought it the other day.

BEATRICE [*to* EDDIE]: They only bought three records. [*She
watches them dance;* EDDIE *turns his head away.* MARCO
just sits there, waiting. Now BEATRICE *turns to* EDDIE.] Must
be nice to go all over in one of them fishin' boats. I would
like that myself. See all them other countries?

EDDIE: Yeah.

BEATRICE [*to* MARCO]: But the women don't go along, I bet.

MARCO: No, not on the boats. Hard work.

BEATRICE: What're you got, a regular kitchen and everything?

MARCO: Yes, we eat very good on the boats – especially when Rodolpho comes along; everybody gets fat.

BEATRICE: Oh, he cooks?

MARCO: Sure, very good cook. Rice, pasta, fish, everything.

[EDDIE *lowers his paper.*]

EDDIE: He's a cook, too! [*Looking at* RODOLPHO] He sings, he cooks ...

[RODOLPHO *smiles thankfully.*]

BEATRICE: Well it's good, he could always make a living.

EDDIE: It's wonderful. He sings, he cooks, he could make dresses ...

CATHERINE: They get some high pay, them guys. The head chefs in all the big hotels are men. You read about them.

EDDIE: That's what I'm sayin'.

[CATHERINE *and* RODOLPHO *continue dancing.*]

CATHERINE: Yeah, well, I mean.

EDDIE [*to* BEATRICE]: He's lucky, believe me. [*Slight pause. He looks away, then back to* BEATRICE.] That's why the water-front is no place for him. [*They stop dancing.* RODOLPHO *turns off phonograph.*] I mean like me – I can't cook, I can't sing, I can't make dresses, so I'm on the water-front. But if I could cook, if I could sing, if I could make dresses, I wouldn't be on the water-front. [*He has been unconsciously twisting the newspaper into a tight roll. They are all regarding him now; he senses he is exposing the issue and he is driven on.*] I would be someplace else. I would be like in a dress store. [*He has bent the rolled paper and it suddenly tears in two. He suddenly gets up and pulls his pants up over his belly and goes to* MARCO.] What do you say, Marco, we go to the bouts next Saturday night. You never seen a fight, did you?

MARCO [*uneasily*]: Only in the moving pictures

EDDIE [*going to* RODOLPHO]: I'll treat yiz. What do you say, Danish? You wanna come along? I'll buy the tickets.

RODOLPHO: Sure. I like to go.

CATHERINE [*goes to* EDDIE; *nervously happy now*]: I'll make some coffee, all right?

EDDIE: Go ahead, make some! Make it nice and strong. [*Mystified, she smiles and exits to kitchen. He is weirdly elated, rubbing his fists into his palms. He strides to* MARCO.] You wait, Marco, you see some real fights here. You ever do any boxing?

MARCO: No, I never.

EDDIE [*to* RODOLPHO]: Betcha you have done some, heh?

RODOLPHO: No.

EDDIE: Well, come on, I'll teach you.

BEATRICE: What's he got to learn that for?

EDDIE: Ya can't tell, one a these days somebody's liable to step on his foot or sump'm. Come on, Rodolpho, I show you a couple a passes. [*He stands below table.*]

BEATRICE: Go ahead, Rodolpho. He's a good boxer, he could teach you.

RODOLPHO [*embarrassed*]: Well, I don't know how to – [*He moves down to* EDDIE.]

EDDIE: Just put your hands up. Like this, see? That's right. That's very good, keep your left up, because you lead with the left, see, like this. [*He gently moves his left into* RODOLPHO's *face.*] See? Now what you gotta do is you gotta block me, so when I come in like that you – [RODOLPHO *parries his left.*] Hey, that's very good! [RODOLPHO *laughs.*] All right, now come into me. Come on.

RODOLPHO: I don't want to hit you, Eddie.

EDDIE: Don't pity me, come on. Throw it, I'll show you how to block it. [RODOLPHO *jabs at him, laughing. The others join.*] 'at's it. Come on again. For the jaw right here. [RODOLPHO *jabs with more assurance.*] Very good!

BEATRICE [*to* MARCO]: He's very good!

[EDDIE *crosses directly upstage of* RODOLPHO.]

EDDIE: Sure, he's great! Come on, kid, put sump'm behind it, you can't hurt me. [RODOLPHO, *more seriously, jabs at* EDDIE's *jaw and grazes it.*] Attaboy.

[CATHERINE *comes from the kitchen, watches.*]

Now I'm gonna hit you, so block me, see?

CATHERINE [*with beginning alarm*]: What are they doin'?

[*They are lightly boxing now.*]

BEATRICE [– *she senses only the comradeship in it now*]: He's teachin' him; he's very good!

EDDIE: Sure, he's terrific! Look at him go! [RODOLPHO *lands a blow.*] 'at's it! Now, watch out, here I come, Danish! [*He feints with his left hand and lands with his right. It mildly staggers* RODOLPHO. MARCO *rises.*]

CATHERINE [*rushing to* RODOLPHO]: Eddie!

EDDIE: Why? I didn't hurt him. Did I hurt you, kid? [*He rubs the back of his hand across his mouth.*]

RODOLPHO: No, no, he didn't hurt me. [*To* EDDIE *with a certain gleam and a smile*] I was only surprised.

BEATRICE [*pulling* EDDIE *down into the rocker*]: That's enough, Eddie; he did pretty good, though.

EDDIE: Yeah. [*Rubbing his fists together*] He could be very good, Marco. I'll teach him again.

[MARCO *nods at him dubiously.*]

RODOLPHO: Dance, Catherine. Come.

[*He takes her hand; they go to phonograph and start it. It plays* Paper Doll.

RODOLPHO *takes her in his arms. They dance.* EDDIE *in thought sits in his chair, and* MARCO *takes a chair, places it in front of* EDDIE, *and looks down at it.* BEATRICE *and* EDDIE *watch him.*]

MARCO: Can you lift this chair?

EDDIE: What do you mean?

MARCO: From here. [*He gets on one knee with one hand behind his back, and grasps the bottom of one of the chair legs but does not raise it.*]

EDDIE: Sure, why not? [*He comes to the chair, kneels, grasps the leg, raises the chair one inch, but it leans over to the floor.*] Gee, that's hard, I never knew that. [*He tries again, and again fails.*] It's on an angle, that's why, heh?

MARCO: Here.

[*He kneels, grasps, and with strain slowly raises the chair higher and higher, getting to his feet now.* RODOLPHO *and* CATHERINE *have stopped dancing as* MARCO *raises the chair over his head.*

MARCO *is face to face with* EDDIE, *a strained tension gripping his eyes and jaw, his neck stiff, the chair raised like a weapon over* EDDIE's *head – and he transforms what might appear like a glare of warning into a smile of triumph, and* EDDIE's *grin vanishes as he absorbs his look.*]

CURTAIN

ACT TWO

[*Light rises on* ALFIERI *at his desk.*]

ALFIERI: On the twenty-third of that December a case of Scotch whisky slipped from a net while being unloaded – as a case of Scotch whisky is inclined to do on the twenty-third of December on Pier Forty-one. There was no snow, but it was cold, his wife was out shopping. Marco was still at work. The boy had not been hired that day; Catherine told me later that this was the first time they had been alone together in the house.

[*Light is rising on* CATHERINE *in the apartment.* RODOLPHO *is watching as she arranges a paper pattern on cloth spread on the table.*]

CATHERINE: You hungry?

RODOLPHO: Not for anything to eat. [*Pause.*] I have nearly three hundred dollars. Catherine?

CATHERINE: I heard you.

RODOLPHO: You don't like to talk about it any more?

CATHERINE: Sure, I don't mind talkin' about it.

RODOLPHO: What worries you, Catherine?

CATHERINE: I been wantin' to ask you about something. Could I?

RODOLPHO: All the answers are in my eyes, Catherine. But you don't look in my eyes lately. You're full of secrets. [*She looks at him. She seems withdrawn.*] What is the question?

CATHERINE: Suppose I wanted to live in Italy.

RODOLPHO [*smiling at the incongruity*]: You going to marry somebody rich?

CATHERINE: No, I mean live there – you and me.

RODOLPHO [*his smile vanishing*]: When?

CATHERINE: Well ... when we get married.

RODOLPHO [*astonished*]: You want to be an Italian?

CATHERINE: No, but I could live there without being Italian. Americans live there.

RODOLPHO: For ever?

CATHERINE: Yeah.

RODOLPHO [*crosses to rocker*]: You're fooling.

CATHERINE: No, I mean it.

RODOLPHO: Where do you get such an idea?

CATHERINE: Well, you're always saying it's so beautiful there, with the mountains and the ocean and all the –

RODOLPHO: You're fooling me.

CATHERINE: I mean it.

RODOLPHO [*goes to her slowly*]: Catherine, if I ever brought you home with no money, no business, nothing, they would call the priest and the doctor and they would say Rodolpho is crazy.

CATHERINE: I know, but I think we would be happier there.

RODOLPHO: Happier! What would you eat? You can't cook the view!

CATHERINE: Maybe you could be a singer, like in Rome or –

RODOLPHO: Rome! Rome is full of singers.

CATHERINE: Well, I could work then.

RODOLPHO: Where?

CATHERINE: God, there must be jobs somewhere!

RODOLPHO: There's nothing! Nothing, nothing, nothing. Now tell me what you're talking about. How can I bring you from a rich country to suffer in a poor country? What are you talking about? [*She searches for words.*] I would be a criminal stealing your face. In two years you would have an old, hungry face. When my brother's babies cry they give them water, water that boiled a bone. Don't you believe that?

CATHERINE [*quietly*]: I'm afraid of Eddie here.

[*Slight pause.*]

RODOLPHO [*steps closer to her*]: We wouldn't live here. Once
I am a citizen I could work anywhere and I would find
better jobs and we would have a house, Catherine. If I were
not afraid to be arrested I would start to be something
wonderful here!

CATHERINE [*steeling herself*]: Tell me something. I mean just
tell me, Rodolpho – would you still want to do it if it
turned out we had to go live in Italy? I mean just if it
turned out that way.

RODOLPHO: This is your question or his question?

CATHERINE: I would like to know, Rodolpho. I mean it.

RODOLPHO: To go there with nothing.

CATHERINE: Yeah.

RODOLPHO: No. [*She looks at him wide-eyed.*] No.

CATHERINE: You wouldn't?

RODOLPHO: No; I will not marry you to live in Italy. I want
you to be my wife, and I want to be a citizen. Tell him that,
or I will. Yes. [*He moves about angrily.*] And tell him also,
and tell yourself, please, that I am not a beggar, and you
are not a horse, a gift, a favour for a poor immigrant.

CATHERINE: Well, don't get mad!

RODOLPHO: I am furious! [*Goes to her.*] Do you think I am
so desperate? My brother is desperate, not me. You think I
would carry on my back the rest of my life a woman I
didn't love just to be an American? It's so wonderful? You
think we have no tall buildings in Italy? Electric lights? No
wide streets? No flags? No automobiles? Only work we
don't have. I want to be an American so I can work, that is
the only wonder here – work! How can you insult me,
Catherine?

CATHERINE: I didn't mean that –

RODOLPHO: My heart dies to look at you. Why are you so
afraid of him?

CATHERINE [*near tears*]: I don't know!

RODOLPHO: Do you trust me, Catherine? You?

CATHERINE: It's only that I – He was good to me, Rodolpho. You don't know him; he was always the sweetest guy to me. Good. He razzes me all the time but he don't mean it. I know. I would – just feel ashamed if I made him sad. 'Cause I always dreamt that when I got married he would be happy at the wedding, and laughin' – and now he's – mad all the time and nasty – [*She is weeping.*] Tell him you'd live in Italy – just tell him, and maybe he would start to trust you a little, see? Because I want him to be happy; I mean – I like him, Rodolpho – and I can't stand it!

RODOLPHO: Oh, Catherine – oh, little girl.

CATHERINE: I love you, Rodolpho, I love you.

RODOLPHO: Then why are you afraid? That he'll spank you?

CATHERINE: Don't, don't laugh at me! I've been here all my life. ... Every day I saw him when he left in the morning and when he came home at night. You think it's so easy to turn around and say to a man he's nothin' to you no more?

RODOLPHO: I know, but –

CATHERINE: You don't know; nobody knows! I'm not a baby, I know a lot more than people think I know. Beatrice says to be a woman, but –

RODOLPHO: Yes.

CATHERINE: Then why don't she be a woman? If I was a wife I would make a man happy instead of goin' at him all the time. I can tell a block away when he's blue in his mind and just wants to talk to somebody quiet and nice. ... I can tell when he's hungry or wants a beer before he even says anything. I know when his feet hurt him, I mean I *know* him and now I'm supposed to turn around and make a stranger out of him? I don't know why I have to do that, I mean.

RODOLPHO: Catherine. If I take in my hands a little bird. And she grows and wishes to fly. But I will not let her out of my hands because I love her so much, is that right for me to do? I don't say you must hate him; but anyway you must go, mustn't you? Catherine?

CATHERINE: [*softly*]: Hold me.

RODOLPHO [*clasping her to him*]: Oh, my little girl.

CATHERINE: Teach me. [*She is weeping.*] I don't know anything, teach me, Rodolpho, hold me.

RODOLPHO: There's nobody here now. Come inside. Come. [*He is leading her towards the bedrooms.*] And don't cry any more.

> [*Light rises on the street. In a moment* EDDIE *appears. He is unsteady, drunk. He mounts the stairs. He enters the apartment, looks around, takes out a bottle from one pocket, puts it on the table. Then another bottle from another pocket, and a third from an inside pocket. He sees the pattern and cloth, goes over to it and touches it, and turns towards upstage.*]

EDDIE: Beatrice? [*He goes to the open kitchen door and looks in.*] Beatrice? Beatrice?

> [CATHERINE *enters from bedroom; under his gaze she adjusts her dress.*]

CATHERINE: You got home early.

EDDIE: Knocked off for Christmas early. [*Indicating the pattern*] Rodolpho makin' you a dress?

CATHERINE: No. I'm makin' a blouse.

> [RODOLPHO *appears in the bedroom doorway.* EDDIE *sees him and his arm jerks slightly in shock.* RODOLPHO *nods to him testingly.*]

RODOLPHO: Beatrice went to buy presents for her mother. [*Pause.*]

EDDIE: Pack it up. Go ahead. Get your stuff and get outa here. [CATHERINE *instantly turns and walks towards the bedroom, and* EDDIE *grabs her arm.*] Where you goin'?

CATHERINE [*trembling with fright*]: I think I have to get out of here, Eddie.

EDDIE: No, you ain't goin' nowheres, he's the one.

CATHERINE: I think I can't stay here no more. [*She frees her arm, steps back towards the bedroom.*] I'm sorry, Eddie. [*She sees the tears in his eyes.*] Well, don't cry. I'll be around the neighbourhood; I'll see you. I just can't stay here no more. You know I can't. [*Her sobs of pity and love for him break her composure.*] Don't you know I can't? You know that, don't you? [*She goes to him.*] Wish me luck. [*She clasps her hands prayerfully.*] Oh, Eddie, don't be like that!

EDDIE: You ain't goin' nowheres.

CATHERINE: Eddie, I'm not gonna be a baby any more! You –

[*He reaches out suddenly, draws her to him, and as she strives to free herself he kisses her on the mouth.*]

RODOLPHO: Don't! [*He pulls on* EDDIE'*s arm.*] Stop that! Have respect for her!

EDDIE [*spun round by* RODOLPHO]: You want something?

RODOLPHO: Yes! She'll be my wife. That is what I want. My wife!

EDDIE: But what're you gonna be?

RODOLPHO: I show you what I be!

CATHERINE: Wait outside; don't argue with him!

EDDIE: Come on, show me! What're you gonna be? Show me!

RODOLPHO [*with tears of rage*]: Don't say that to me!

[RODOLPHO *flies at him in attack.* EDDIE *pins his arms, laughing, and suddenly kisses him.*]

CATHERINE: Eddie! Let go, ya hear me! I'll kill you! Leggo of him!

[*She tears at* EDDIE'*s face and* EDDIE *releases* RODOLPHO. EDDIE *stands there with tears rolling down his face as he laughs mockingly at* RODOLPHO. *She is staring at him in horror.*

RODOLPHO *is rigid. They are like animals that have torn at one another and broken up without a decision, each waiting for the other's mood.*]

EDDIE [*to* CATHERINE]: You see? [*To* RODOLPHO] I give you till tomorrow, kid. Get outa here. Alone. You hear me? Alone.

CATHERINE: I'm going with him, Eddie. [*She starts towards* RODOLPHO.]

EDDIE [*indicating* RODOLPHO *with his head*]: Not with that. [*She halts, frightened. He sits, still panting for breath, and they watch him helplessly as he leans towards them over the table.*] Don't make me do nuttin', Catherine. Watch your step, submarine. By rights they oughta throw you back in the water. But I got pity for you. [*He moves unsteadily towards the door, always facing* RODOLPHO.] Just get outa here and don't lay another hand on her unless you wanna go out feet first.

[*He goes out of the apartment.*

The lights go down, as they rise on ALFIERI.]

ALFIERI: On December twenty-seventh I saw him next. I normally go home well before six, but that day I sat around looking out my window at the bay, and when I saw him walking through my doorway, I knew why I had waited. And if I seem to tell this like a dream, it was that way. Several moments arrived in the course of the two talks we had when it occurred to me how – almost transfixed I had come to feel. I had lost my strength somewhere. [EDDIE *enters, removing his cap, sits in the chair, looks thoughtfully out.*] I looked in his eyes more than I listened – in fact, I can hardly remember the conversation. But I will never forget how dark the room became when he looked at me; his eyes were like tunnels. I kept wanting to call the police, but nothing had happened. Nothing at all had really happened. [*He breaks off and looks down at the desk. Then he turns to* EDDIE.] So in other words, he won't leave?

EDDIE: My wife is talkin' about renting a room upstairs for them. An old lady on the top floor is got an empty room.

ALFIERI: What does Marco say?

EDDIE: He just sits there. Marco don't say much.

ALFIERI: I guess they didn't tell him, heh? What happened?

EDDIE: I don't know; Marco don't say much.

ALFIERI: What does your wife say?

EDDIE [*unwilling to pursue this*]: Nobody's talkin' much in the house. So what about that?

ALFIERI: But you didn't prove anything about him. It sounds like he just wasn't strong enough to break your grip.

EDDIE: I'm tellin' you I know – he ain't right. Somebody that don't want it can break it. Even a mouse, if you catch a teeny mouse and you hold it in your hand, that mouse can give you the right kind of fight. He didn't give me the right kind of fight, I know it, Mr Alfieri, the guy ain't right.

ALFIERI: What did you do that for, Eddie?

EDDIE: To show her what he is! So she would see, once and for all! Her mother'll turn over in the grave! [*He gathers himself almost peremptorily.*] So what do I gotta do now? Tell me what to do.

ALFIERI: She actually said she's marrying him?

EDDIE: She told me, yeah. So what do I do?

[*Slight pause.*]

ALFIERI: This is my last word, Eddie, take it or not, that's your business. Morally and legally you have no rights, you cannot stop it; she is a free agent.

EDDIE [*angering*]: Didn't you hear what I told you?

ALFIERI [*with a tougher tone*]: I heard what you told me, and I'm telling you what the answer is. I'm not only telling you now, I'm warning you – the law is nature. The law is only a word for what has a right to happen. When the law is wrong it's because it's unnatural, but in this case it is natural and a river will drown you if you buck it now. Let her go.

And bless her. [*A phone booth begins to glow on the opposite side of the stage; a faint, lonely blue.* EDDIE *stands up, jaws clenched.*] Somebody had to come for her, Eddie, sooner or later. [EDDIE *starts turning to go and* ALFIERI *rises with new anxiety.*] You won't have a friend in the world, Eddie! Even those who understand will turn against you, even the ones who feel the same will despise you! [EDDIE *moves off.*] Put it out of your mind! Eddie!

[*He follows into the darkness, calling desperately.*

EDDIE *is gone. The phone is glowing in light now. Light is out on* ALFIERI. EDDIE *has at the same time appeared beside the phone.*]

EDDIE: Give me the number of the Immigration Bureau. Thanks. [*He dials.*] I want to report something. Illegal immigrants. Two of them. That's right. 441 Saxon Street, Brooklyn, yeah. Ground floor. Heh? [*With greater difficulty*] I'm just around the neighbourhood, that's all. Heh?

[*Evidently he is being questioned further, and he slowly hangs up. He leaves the phone just as* LOUIS *and* MIKE *come down the street.*]

LOUIS: Go bowlin', Eddie?

EDDIE: No, I'm due home.

LOUIS: Well, take it easy.

EDDIE: I'll see yiz.

[*They leave him, exiting right, and he watches them go. He glances about, then goes up into the house. The lights go on in the apartment.* BEATRICE *is taking down Christmas decorations and packing them in a box.*]

EDDIE: Where is everybody? [BEATRICE *does not answer.*] I says where is everybody?

BEATRICE [*looking up at him, wearied with it, and concealing a fear of him*]: I decided to move them upstairs with Mrs Dondero.

EDDIE: Oh, they're all moved up there already?

BEATRICE: Yeah.

EDDIE: Where's Catherine? She up there?

BEATRICE: Only to bring pillow-cases.

EDDIE: She ain't movin' in with them.

BEATRICE: Look, I'm sick and tired of it. I'm sick and tired of it!

EDDIE: All right, all right, take it easy.

BEATRICE: I don't wanna hear no more about it, you understand? Nothin'!

EDDIE: What're you blowin' off about? Who brought them in here?

BEATRICE: All right, I'm sorry; I wish I'd a drop dead before I told them to come. In the ground I wish I was.

EDDIE: Don't drop dead, just keep in mind who brought them in here, that's all. [*He moves about restlessly.*] I mean I got a couple of rights here. [*He moves, wanting to beat down her evident disapproval of him.*] This is my house here not their house.

BEATRICE: What do you want from me? They're moved out; what do you want now?

EDDIE: I want my respect!

BEATRICE: So I moved them out, what more do you want? You got your house now, you got your respect.

EDDIE [– *he moves about biting his lip*]: I don't like the way you talk to me, Beatrice.

BEATRICE: I'm just tellin' you I done what you want!

EDDIE: I don't like it! The way you talk to me and the way you look at me. This is my house. And she is my niece and I'm responsible for her.

BEATRICE: So that's why you done that to him?

EDDIE: I done what to him?

BEATRICE: What you done to him in front of her; you know what I'm talkin' about. She goes around shakin' all the time, she can't go to sleep! That's what you call responsible for her?

EDDIE [*quietly*]: The guy ain't right, Beatrice. [*She is silent.*] Did you hear what I said?

BEATRICE: Look, I'm finished with it. That's all. [*She resumes her work.*]

EDDIE [*helping her to pack the tinsel*]: I'm gonna have it out with you one of these days, Beatrice.

BEATRICE: Nothin' to have out with me, it's all settled. Now we gonna be like it never happened, that's all.

EDDIE: I want my respect, Beatrice, and you know what I'm talkin' about.

BEATRICE: What?

[*Pause.*]

EDDIE [– *finally his resolution hardens*]: What I feel like doin' in the bed and what I don't feel like doin'. I don't want no –

BEATRICE: When'd I say anything about that?

EDDIE: You said, you said, I ain't deaf. I don't want no more conversations about that, Beatrice. I do what I feel like doin' or what I don't feel like doin'.

BEATRICE: Okay.

[*Pause.*]

EDDIE: You used to be different, Beatrice. You had a whole different way.

BEATRICE: *I'm* no different.

EDDIE: You didn't used to jump me all the time about everything. The last year or two I come in the house I don't know what's gonna hit me. It's a shootin' gallery in here and I'm the pigeon.

BEATRICE: Okay, okay.

EDDIE: Don't tell me okay, okay, I'm tellin' you the truth. A wife is supposed to believe the husband. If I tell you that guy ain't right don't tell me he is right.

BEATRICE: But how do you know?

EDDIE: Because I know. I don't go around makin' accusations. He give me the heeby-jeebies the first minute I seen him.

And I don't like you sayin' I don't want her marryin' anybody. I broke my back payin' her stenography lessons so she could go out and meet a better class of people. Would I do that if I didn't want her to get married? Sometimes you talk like I was a crazy man or sump'm.

BEATRICE: But she likes him.

EDDIE: Beatrice, she's a baby, how is she gonna know what she likes?

BEATRICE: Well, you kept her a baby, you wouldn't let her go out. I told you a hundred times.

[Pause.]

EDDIE: All right. Let her go out, then.

BEATRICE: She don't wanna go out now. It's too late, Eddie.

[Pause.]

EDDIE: Suppose I told her to go out. Suppose I –

BEATRICE: They're going to get married next week, Eddie.

EDDIE [– his head jerks around to her]: She said that?

BEATRICE: Eddie, if you want my advice, go to her and tell her good luck. I think maybe now that you had it out you learned better.

EDDIE: What's the hurry next week?

BEATRICE: Well, she's been worried about him bein' picked up; this way he could start to be a citizen. She loves him, Eddie. [He gets up, moves about uneasily, restlessly.] Why don't you give her a good word? Because I still think she would like you to be a friend, y'know? [He is standing, looking at the floor.] I mean like if you told her you'd go to the wedding.

EDDIE: She asked you that?

BEATRICE: I know she would like it. I'd like to make a party here for her. I mean there oughta be some kinda send-off. Heh? I mean she'll have trouble enough in her life, let's start it off happy. What do you say? 'Cause in her heart she still loves you, Eddie. I know it. [He presses his fingers against *his eyes.*] What're you, cryin'? [*She goes to him, holds his face.*] Go...whyn't you go tell her you're sorry? [CATHERINE *is seen on the upper landing of the stairway, and they hear her descending.*] There ... she's comin' down. Come on, shake hands with her.

EDDIE [*moving with suppressed suddenness*]: No, I can't, I can't talk to her.

BEATRICE: Eddie, give her a break; a wedding should be happy!

EDDIE: I'm goin', I'm goin' for a walk.

[*He goes upstage for his jacket.* CATHERINE *enters and starts for the bedroom door.*]

BEATRICE: Katie? . . . Eddie, don't go, wait a minute. [*She embraces* EDDIE's *arm with warmth.*] Ask him, Katie. Come on, honey.

EDDIE: It's all right, I'm – [*He starts to go and she holds him.*]

BEATRICE: No, she wants to ask you. Come on, Katie, ask him. We'll have a party! What're we gonna do, hate each other? Come on!

CATHERINE: I'm gonna get married, Eddie. So if you wanna come, the wedding be on Saturday.

[*Pause.*]

EDDIE: Okay. I only wanted the best for you, Katie. I hope you know that.

CATHERINE: Okay. [*She starts out again.*]

EDDIE: Catherine? [*She turns to him.*] I was just tellin' Beatrice ... if you wanna go out, like ... I mean I realize maybe I kept you home too much. Because he's the first guy you ever knew, y'know? I mean now that you got a job, you might meet some fellas, and you get a different idea, y'know? I mean you could always come back to him, you're still only kids, the both of yiz. What's the hurry? Maybe you'll get around a little bit, you grow up a little more, maybe you'll see different in a couple of months. I mean you be surprised, it don't have to be him.

CATHERINE: No, we made it up already.

EDDIE [with increasing anxiety]: Katie, wait a minute.

CATHERINE: No, I made up my mind.

EDDIE: But you never knew no other fella, Katie! How could you make up your mind?

CATHERINE: 'Cause I did. I don't want nobody else.

EDDIE: But, Katie, suppose he gets picked up.

CATHERINE: That's why we gonna do it right away. Soon as we finish the wedding he's goin' right over and start to be a citizen. I made up my mind, Eddie. I'm sorry. [To BEATRICE] Could I take two more pillow-cases for the other guys?

BEATRICE: Sure, go ahead. Only don't let her forget where they came from.

[CATHERINE goes into a bedroom.]

EDDIE: She's got other boarders up there?

BEATRICE: Yeah, there's two guys that just came over.

EDDIE: What do you mean, came over?

BEATRICE: From Italy. Lipari the butcher – his nephew. They come from Bari, they just got here yesterday. I didn't even know till Marco and Rodolpho moved up there before. [CATHERINE enters, going towards exit with two pillow-cases.] It'll be nice, they could all talk together.

EDDIE: Catherine! [She halts near the exit door. He takes in BEATRICE too.] What're you, got no brains? You put them up there with two other submarines?

CATHERINE: Why?

EDDIE [in a driving fright and anger]: Why! How do you know they're not trackin' these guys? They'll come up for them and find Marco and Rodolpho! Get them out of the house!

BEATRICE: But they been here so long already –

EDDIE: How do you know what enemies Lipari's got? Which they'd love to stab him in the back?

CATHERINE: Well what'll I do with them?

EDDIE: The neighbourhood is full of rooms. Can't you stand to live a couple of blocks away from him? Get them out of the house!

CATHERINE: Well maybe tomorrow night I'll –

EDDIE: Not tomorrow, do it now. Catherine, you never mix yourself with somebody else's family! These guys get picked up, Lipari's liable to blame you or me and we got his whole family on our head. They got a temper, that family.

[*Two men in overcoats appear outside, start into the house.*]

CATHERINE: How'm I gonna find a place tonight?

EDDIE: Will you stop arguin' with me and get them out! You think I'm always tryin' to fool you or sump'm? What's the matter with you, don't you believe I could think of your good? Did I ever ask sump'm for myself? You think I got no feelin's? I never told you nothin' in my life that wasn't for your own good. Nothin'! And look at the way you talk to me! Like I was an enemy! Like I – [*A knock on the door. His head swerves. They all stand motionless. Another knock.* EDDIE, *in a whisper, pointing upstage.*] Go up the fire escape, get them out over the back fence.

[CATHERINE *stands motionless, uncomprehending.*]

FIRST OFFICER [*in the hall*]: Immigration! Open up in there!

EDDIE: Go, go. Hurry up! [*She stands a moment staring at him in a realized horror.*] Well, what're you lookin' at!

FIRST OFFICER: Open up!

EDDIE [*calling towards the door*]: Who's that there?

FIRST OFFICER: Immigration, open up.

[EDDIE *turns, looks at* BEATRICE. *She sits. Then he looks at* CATHERINE. *With a sob of fury* CATHERINE *streaks into a bedroom.*
Knock is repeated.]

EDDIE: All right, take it easy, take it easy. [*He goes and opens the door. The* OFFICER *steps inside.*] What's all this?

FIRST OFFICER: Where are they?

[SECOND OFFICER *sweeps past and, glancing about, goes into the kitchen.*]

EDDIE: Where's who?

FIRST OFFICER: Come on, come on, where are they? [*He hurries into the bedrooms.*]

EDDIE: Who? We got nobody here. [*He looks at* BEATRICE, *who turns her head away. Pugnaciously, furious, he steps towards* BEATRICE.] What's the matter with *you*?

[FIRST OFFICER *enters from the bedroom, calls to the kitchen.*]

FIRST OFFICER: Dominick?

[*Enter* SECOND OFFICER *from kitchen.*]

SECOND OFFICER: Maybe it's a different apartment.

FIRST OFFICER: There's only two more floors up there. I'll take the front, you go up the fire escape. I'll let you in. Watch your step up there.

SECOND OFFICER: Okay, right, Charley. [FIRST OFFICER *goes out apartment door and runs up the stairs.*] This is 441, isn't it?

EDDIE: That's right.

[SECOND OFFICER *goes out into the kitchen.*

EDDIE *turns to* BEATRICE. *She looks at him now and sees his terror.*]

BEATRICE [*weakened with fear*]: Oh, Jesus, Eddie.

EDDIE: What's the matter with *you*?

BEATRICE [*pressing her palms against her face*]: Oh, my God, my God.

EDDIE: What're you, accusin' me?

BEATRICE [– *her final thrust is to turn towards him instead of running from him*]: My God, what did you do?

[*Many steps on the outer stair draw his attention. We see the* FIRST OFFICER *descending, with* MARCO, *behind him* RODOLPHO, *and* CATHERINE, *and the two strange immi-*

grants, followed by SECOND OFFICER. BEATRICE *hurries to door.*]

CATHERINE [*backing down stairs, fighting with* FIRST OFFICER; *as they appear on the stairs*]: What do yiz want from them? They work, that's all. They're boarders upstairs, they work on the piers.

BEATRICE [*to* FIRST OFFICER]: Ah, Mister, what do you want from them, who do they hurt?

CATHERINE [*pointing to* RODOLPHO]: They ain't no submarines, he was born in Philadelphia.

FIRST OFFICER: Step aside, lady.

CATHERINE: What do you mean? You can't just come in a house and –

FIRST OFFICER: All right, take it easy. [*To* RODOLPHO] What street were you born in Philadelphia?

CATHERINE: What do you mean, what street? Could you tell me what street you were born?

FIRST OFFICER: Sure. Four blocks away, 111 Union Street. Let's go fellas.

CATHERINE [*fending him off* RODOLPHO]: No, you can't! Now, get outa here!

FIRST OFFICER: Look, girlie, if they're all right they'll be out tomorrow. If they're illegal they go back where they came from. If you want, get yourself a lawyer, although I'm tellin' you now you're wasting your money. Let's get them in the car, Dom. [*To the men*] Andiamo, andiamo, let's go.

[*The men start, but* MARCO *hangs back.*]

BEATRICE [*from doorway*]: Who're they hurtin', for God's sake, what do you want from them? They're starvin' over there, what do you want! Marco!

[MARCO *suddenly breaks from the group and dashes into the room and faces* EDDIE; BEATRICE *and* FIRST OFFICER *rush in as* MARCO *spits into* EDDIE's *face.*

CATHERINE *runs into hallway and throws herself into* RODOLPHO's *arms.* EDDIE, *with an enraged cry, lunges for* MARCO.]

EDDIE: Oh, you mother's – !

[FIRST OFFICER *quickly intercedes and pushes* EDDIE *from* MARCO, *who stands there accusingly.*]

FIRST OFFICER [*between them, pushing* EDDIE *from* MARCO]: Cut it out!

EDDIE [*over the* FIRST OFFICER's *shoulder, to* MARCO]: I'll kill you for that, you son of a bitch!

FIRST OFFICER: Hey! [*Shakes him.*] Stay in here now, don't come out, don't bother him. You hear me? Don't come out, fella.

[*For an instant there is silence. Then* FIRST OFFICER *turns and takes* MARCO's *arm and then gives a last, informative look at* EDDIE. *As he and* MARCO *are going out into the hall,* EDDIE *erupts.*]

EDDIE: I don't forget that, Marco! You hear what I'm sayin'?

[*Out in the hall,* FIRST OFFICER *and* MARCO *go down the stairs. Now, in the street,* LOUIS, MIKE, *and several neighbours including the butcher,* LIPARI – *a stout, intense, middle-aged man* – *are gathering around the stoop.*

LIPARI, *the butcher, walks over to the two strange men and kisses them. His wife, keening, goes and kisses their hands.*

EDDIE *is emerging from the house shouting after* MARCO.

BEATRICE *is trying to restrain him.*]

EDDIE: That's the thanks I get? Which I took the blankets off my bed for yiz? You gonna apologize to me, Marco! *Marco!*

FIRST OFFICER [*in the doorway with* MARCO]: All right, lady, let them go. Get in the car, fellas, it's right over there.

[RODOLPHO *is almost carrying the sobbing* CATHERINE *off up the street, left.*]

CATHERINE: He was born in Philadelphia! What do you want from him?

FIRST OFFICER: Step aside, lady, come on now …

> [*The* SECOND OFFICER *has moved off with the two strange men.* MARCO, *taking advantage of the* FIRST OFFICER'S *being occupied with* CATHERINE, *suddenly frees himself and points back at* EDDIE.]

MARCO: That one! I accuse that one!

> [EDDIE *brushes* BEATRICE *aside and rushes out to the stoop.*]

FIRST OFFICER [*grabbing him and moving him quickly off up the left street*]: Come on!

MARCO [*as he is taken off, pointing back at* EDDIE]: That one! He killed my children! That one stole the food from my children!

> [MARCO *is gone. The crowd has turned to* EDDIE.]

EDDIE [*to* LIPARI *and wife*]: He's crazy! I give them the blankets off my bed. Six months I kept them like my own brothers!

> [LIPARI, *the butcher, turns and starts up left with his arm around his wife.*]

EDDIE: Lipari! [*He follows* LIPARI *up left.*] For Christ's sake, I kept them, I give them the blankets off my bed!

> [LIPARI *and wife exit.* EDDIE *turns and starts crossing down right to* LOUIS *and* MIKE.]

EDDIE: Louis! *Louis!*

> [LOUIS *barely turns, then walks off and exits down right with* MIKE. *Only* BEATRICE *is left on the stoop.* CATHERINE *now returns, blank-eyed, from offstage and the car.* EDDIE *calls after* LOUIS *and* MIKE.]

EDDIE: He's gonna take that back. He's gonna take that back or I'll kill him! You hear me? I'll kill him! I'll kill him!

> [*He exits up street calling.*
> There is a pause of darkness before the lights rise, on the reception room of a prison.* MARCO *is seated;* ALFIERI, CATHERINE, *and* RODOLPHO *standing.*]

ALFIERI: I'm waiting, Marco, what do you say?

RODOLPHO: Marco never hurt anybody.

ALFIERI: I can bail you out until your hearing comes up. But I'm not going to do it, you understand me? Unless I have your promise. You're an honourable man, I will believe your promise. Now what do you say?

MARCO: In my country he would be dead now. He would not live this long.

ALFIERI: All right, Rodolpho – you come with me now.

RODOLPHO: No! Please, Mister. Marco – promise the man. Please, I want you to watch the wedding. How can I be married and you're in here? Please, you're not going to do anything; you know you're not.

[MARCO *is silent.*]

CATHERINE [*kneeling left of* MARCO]: Marco, don't you understand? He can't bail you out if you're gonna do something bad. To hell with Eddie. Nobody is gonna talk to him again if he lives to a hundred. Everybody knows you spit in his face, that's enough, isn't it? Give me the satisfaction – I want you at the wedding. You got a wife and kids, Marco. You could be workin' till the hearing comes up, instead of layin' around here.

MARCO [*to* ALFIERI]: I have no chance?

ALFIERI [*crosses to behind* MARCO]: No, Marco. You're going back. The hearing is a formality, that's all.

MARCO: But him? There is a chance, eh?

ALFIERI: When she marries him he can start to become an American. They permit that, if the wife is born here.

MARCO [*looking at* RODOLPHO]: Well – we did something. [*He lays a palm on* RODOLPHO'*s arm and* RODOLPHO *covers it.*]

RODOLPHO: Marco, tell the man.

MARCO [*pulling his hand away*]: What will I tell him? He knows such a promise is dishonourable.

ALFIERI: To promise not to kill is not dishonourable.

MARCO [*looking at* ALFIERI]: No?

ALFIERI: No.

MARCO [*gesturing with his head – this is a new idea*]: Then what is done with such a man?

ALFIERI: Nothing. If he obeys the law, he lives. That's all.

MARCO [*rises, turns to* ALFIERI]: The law? All the law is not in a book.

ALFIERI: Yes. In a book. There is no other law.

MARCO [*his anger rising*]: He degraded my brother. My blood. He robbed my children, he mocks my work. I work to come here, mister!

ALFIERI: I know, Marco –

MARCO: There is no law for that? Where is the law for that?

ALFIERI: There is none.

MARCO [*shaking his head, sitting*]: I don't understand this country.

ALFIERI: Well? What is your answer? You have five or six weeks you could work. Or else you sit here. What do you say to me?

MARCO [*lowers his eyes. It almost seems he is ashamed*]: All right.

ALFIERI: You won't touch him. This is your promise.

[*Slight pause.*]

MARCO: Maybe he wants to apologize to me.

[MARCO *is staring away.* ALFIERI *takes one of his hands.*]

ALFIERI: This is not God, Marco. You hear? Only God makes justice.

MARCO: All right.

ALFIERI [*nodding, not with assurance*]: Good! Catherine, Rodolpho, Marco, let us go.

[CATHERINE *kisses* RODOLPHO *and* MARCO, *then kisses* ALFIERI's *hand*]

CATHERINE: I'll get Beatrice and meet you at the church.

[*She leaves quickly.*

MARCO *rises.* RODOLPHO *suddenly embraces him.* MARCO

pats him on the back and RODOLPHO *exits after* CATHER-
INE. MARCO *faces* ALFIERI.]

ALFIERI: Only God, Marco.

[MARCO *turns and walks out.* ALFIERI *with a certain proces-
sional tread leaves the stage. The lights dim out.*

The lights rise in the apartment. EDDIE *is alone in the rocker,
rocking back and forth in little surges. Pause. Now* BEATRICE
emerges from a bedroom. She is in her best clothes, wearing a hat.]

BEATRICE [*with fear, going to* EDDIE]: I'll be back in about an
hour, Eddie. All right?

EDDIE [*quietly, almost inaudibly, as though drained*]: What, have
I been talkin' to myself?

BEATRICE: Eddie, for God's sake, it's her wedding.

EDDIE: Didn't you hear what I told you? You walk out that
door to that wedding you ain't comin' back here, Beatrice.

BEATRICE: Why! What do you want?

EDDIE: I want my respect. Didn't you ever hear of that? From
my wife?

[CATHERINE *enters from bedroom.*]

CATHERINE: It's after three; we're supposed to be there
already, Beatrice. The priest won't wait.

BEATRICE: Eddie. It's her wedding. There'll be nobody there
from her family. For my sister let me go. I'm goin' for my
sister.

EDDIE [*as though hurt*]: Look, I been arguin' with you all day
already, Beatrice, and I said what I'm gonna say. He's gonna
come here and apologize to me or nobody from this house
is goin' into that church today. Now if that's more to you
than I am, then go. But don't come back. You be on my
side or on their side, that's all.

CATHERINE [*suddenly*]: Who the hell do you think you are?

BEATRICE: Sssh!

CATHERINE: You got no more right to tell nobody nothin'!
Nobody! The rest of your life, nobody!

BEATRICE: Shut up, Katie. [*She turns* CATHERINE *around.*]

CATHERINE: You're gonna come with me!

BEATRICE: I can't, Katie, I can't …

CATHERINE: How can you listen to him? This rat!

BEATRICE [*shaking* CATHERINE]: Don't you call him that!

CATHERINE [*clearing from* BEATRICE]: What're you scared of?
He's a rat! He belongs in the sewer!

BEATRICE: Stop it!

CATHERINE [*weeping*]: He bites people when they sleep! He
comes when nobody's lookin' and poisons decent people.
In the garbage he belongs!

[EDDIE *seems about to pick up the table and fling it at her.*]

BEATRICE: No, Eddie! Eddie! [*To* CATHERINE] Then we
all belong in the garbage. You, and me too. Don't say that.
Whatever happened we all done it, and don't you ever
forget it, Catherine. [*She goes to* CATHERINE.] Now go, go
to your wedding, Katie, I'll stay home. Go. God bless you,
God bless your children.

[*Enter* RODOLPHO.]

RODOLPHO: Eddie?

EDDIE: Who said you could come in here? Get outa here!

RODOLPHO: Marco is coming, Eddie. [*Pause.* BEATRICE
raises her hands in terror.] He's praying in the church. You
understand? [*Pause.* RODOLPHO *advances in the room.*]
Catherine, I think it is better we go. Come with me.

CATHERINE: Eddie, go away please.

BEATRICE [*quietly*]: Eddie. Let's go someplace. Come. You
and me. [*He has not moved.*] I don't want you to be here
when he comes. I'll get your coat.

EDDIE: Where? Where am I goin'? This is my house.

BEATRICE [*crying out*]: What's the use of it! He's crazy now,
you know the way they get, what good is it! You got
nothin' against Marco, you always liked Marco!

EDDIE: I got nothin' against Marco? Which he called me a rat in front of the whole neighbourhood? Which he said I killed his children! Where you been?

RODOLPHO [*quite suddenly, stepping up to* EDDIE]: It is my fault, Eddie. Everything. I wish to apologize. It was wrong that I do not ask your permission. I kiss your hand. [*He reaches for* EDDIE'*s hand, but* EDDIE *snaps it away from him.*]

BEATRICE: Eddie, he's apologizing!

RODOLPHO: I have made all our troubles. But you have insult me too. Maybe God understand why you did that to me. Maybe you did not mean to insult me at all –

BEATRICE: Listen to him! Eddie, listen what he's tellin' you!

RODOLPHO: I think, maybe when Marco comes, if we can tell him we are comrades now, and we have no more argument between us. Then maybe Marco will not –

EDDIE: Now, listen –

CATHERINE: Eddie, give him a chance!

BEATRICE: What do you want! Eddie, what do you want!

EDDIE: I want my name! He didn't take my name; he's only a punk. Marco's got my name – [*to* RODOLPHO] and you can run tell him, kid, that he's gonna give it back to me in front of this neighbourhood, or we have it out. [*Hoisting up his pants*] Come on, where is he? Take me to him.

BEATRICE: Eddie, listen –

EDDIE: I heard enough! Come on, let's go!

BEATRICE: Only blood is good? He kissed your hand!

EDDIE: What he does don't mean nothin' to nobody! [*To* RODOLPHO] Come on!

BEATRICE [*barring his way to the stairs*]: What's gonna mean somethin'? Eddie, listen to me. Who could give you your name? Listen to me, I love you, I'm talkin' to you, I love you; if Marco'll kiss your hand outside, if he goes on his knees, what is he got to give you? That's not what you want.

EDDIE: Don't bother me!

BEATRICE: You want somethin' else, Eddie, and you can never have her!

CATHERINE [*in horror*]: B.!

EDDIE [*shocked, horrified, his fists clenching*]: Beatrice!

[MARCO *appears outside, walking towards the door from a distant point.*]

BEATRICE [*crying out, weeping*]: The truth is not as bad as blood, Eddie! I'm tellin' you the truth – tell her good-bye for ever!

EDDIE [*crying out in agony*]: That's what you think of me – that I would have such a thoughts? [*His fists clench his head as though it will burst.*]

MARCO [*calling near the door outside*]: Eddie Carbone!

[EDDIE *swerves about; all stand transfixed for an instant. People appear outside.*]

EDDIE [*as though flinging his challenge*]: Yeah, Marco! Eddie Carbone. Eddie Carbone. Eddie Carbone. [*He goes up the stairs and emerges from the apartment.* RODOLPHO *streaks up and out past him and runs to* MARCO.]

RODOLPHO: No, Marco, please! Eddie, please, he has children! You will kill a family!

BEATRICE: Go in the house! Eddie, go in the house!

EDDIE [– *he gradually comes to address the people*]: Maybe he come to apologize to me. Heh, Marco? For what you said about me in front of the neighbourhood? [*He is incensing himself and little bits of laughter even escape him as his eyes are murderous and he cracks his knuckles in his hands with a strange sort of relaxation.*] He knows that ain't right. To do like that? To a man? Which I put my roof over their head and my food in their mouth? Like in the Bible? Strangers I never seen in my whole life? To come out of the water and grab a girl for a passport? To go and take from your own family like from the stable – and never a word to me? And now accusations in the bargain! [*Directly to* MARCO]

Wipin' the neighbourhood with my name like a dirty rag! I want my name, Marco. [*He is moving now, carefully, towards* MARCO.] Now gimme my name and we go together to the wedding.

BEATRICE *and* CATHERINE [*keening*]: Eddie! Eddie, don't! Eddie!

EDDIE: No, Marco knows what's right from wrong. Tell the people, Marco, tell them what a liar you are! [*He has his arms spread and* MARCO *is spreading his.*] Come on, liar, you know what you done!

> [*He lunges for* MARCO *as a great hushed shout goes up from the people.*
>
> MARCO *strikes* EDDIE *beside the neck.*]

MARCO: Animal! You go on your knees to me!

> [EDDIE *goes down with the blow and* MARCO *starts to raise a foot to stomp him when* EDDIE *springs a knife into his hand and* MARCO *steps back.* LOUIS *rushes in towards* EDDIE.]

LOUIS: Eddie, for Christ's sake!

> [EDDIE *raises the knife and* LOUIS *halts and steps back.*]

EDDIE: You lied about me, Marco. Now say it. Come on now, say it!

MARCO: Anima-a-a-l!

> [EDDIE *lunges with the knife.* MARCO *grabs his arm, turning the blade inward and pressing it home as the women and* LOUIS *and* MIKE *rush in and separate them, and* EDDIE, *the knife still in his hand, falls to his knees before* MARCO. *The two women support him for a moment, calling his name again and again.*]

CATHERINE: Eddie, I never meant to do nothing bad to you.

EDDIE: Then why – Oh, B.!

BEATRICE: Yes, yes!

EDDIE: My B.!

> [*He dies in her arms, and* BEATRICE *covers him with her body.* ALFIERI, *who is in the crowd, turns out to the audience.*

The lights have gone down, leaving him in a glow, while behind him the dull prayers of the people and the keening of the women continue.]

ALFIERI: Most of the time now we settle for half and I like it better. But the truth is holy, and even as I know how wrong he was, and his death useless, I tremble, for I confess that something perversely pure calls to me from his memory – not purely good, but himself purely, for he allowed himself to be wholly known and for that I think I will love him more than all my sensible clients. And yet, it is better to settle for half, it must be! And so I mourn him – I admit it – with a certain ... alarm.

CURTAIN

ALL MY SONS

CHARACTERS OF THE PLAY

JOE KELLER

KATE KELLER

CHRIS KELLER

ANN DEEVER

GEORGE DEEVER

DR JIM BAYLISS

SUE BAYLISS

FRANK LUBEY

LYDIA LUBEY

BERT

ACT ONE

The back yard of the Keller home in the outskirts of an American town. August of our era.

The stage is hedged on right and left by tall, closely planted poplars which lend the yard a secluded atmosphere. Upstage is filled with the back of the house and its open, unroofed porch which extends into the yard some six feet. The house is two storeys high and has seven rooms. It would have cost perhaps fifteen thousand in the early twenties when it was built. Now it is nicely painted, looks tight and comfortable, and the yard is green with sod, here and there plants whose season is gone. At the right, beside the house, the entrance of the driveway can be seen, but the poplars cut off view of its continuation downstage. In the left corner, downstage, stands the four-foot-high stump of a slender apple-tree whose upper trunk and branches lie toppled beside it, fruit still clinging to its branches.

Downstage right is a small, trellised arbour, shaped like a sea shell, with a decorative bulb hanging from its forward-curving roof. Garden chairs and a table are scattered about. A garbage pail on the ground next to the porch steps, a wire leaf-burner near it.

On the rise; it is early Sunday morning. JOE KELLER *is sitting in the sun reading the want ads of the Sunday paper, the other sections of which lie neatly on the ground beside him. Behind his back, inside the arbour,* DOCTOR JIM BAYLISS *is reading part of the paper at the table.*

KELLER *is nearing sixty. A heavy man of stolid mind and build, a business man these many years, but with the imprint of the machine-shop worker and boss still upon him. When he reads, when he speaks, when he listens, it is with the terrible concentration of the uneducated man for whom there is still wonder in many commonly known things, a man whose judgements must be dredged out of*

experience and a peasant-like common sense. A man among men.
DOCTOR BAYLISS *is nearly forty. A wry self-controlled man, an easy talker, but with a wisp of sadness that clings even to his self-effacing humour.*

[*At curtain,* JIM *is standing at left, staring at the broken tree. He taps a pipe on it, blows through the pipe, feels in his pockets for tobacco, then speaks.*]

JIM: Where's your tobacco?
KELLER: I think I left it on the table. [JIM *goes slowly to table on the arbour, finds a pouch, and sits there on the bench, filling his pipe.*] Gonna rain tonight.
JIM: Paper says so?
KELLER: Yeah, right here.
JIM: Then it can't rain.

[FRANK LUBEY *enters, through a small space between the poplars.* FRANK *is thirty-two but balding. A pleasant, opinionated man, uncertain of himself, with a tendency towards peevishness when crossed, but always wanting it pleasant and neighbourly. He rather saunters in, leisurely, nothing to do. He does not notice* JIM *in the arbour. On his greeting,* JIM *does not bother looking up.*]

FRANK: Hya.
KELLER: Hello, Frank. What's doin'?
FRANK: Nothin'. Walking off my breakfast. [*Looks up at the sky.*] That beautiful? Not a cloud.
KELLER [*looking up*]: Yeah, nice.
FRANK: Every Sunday ought to be like this.
KELLER [*indicating the sections beside him*]: Want the paper?
FRANK: What's the difference, it's all bad news. What's today's calamity?
KELLER: I don't know, I don't read the news part any more. It's more interesting in the want ads.
FRANK: Why, you trying to buy something?

KELLER: No, I'm just interested. To see what people want, y'know? For instance, here's a guy is lookin' for two New-foundland dogs. Now what's he want with two Newfound-land dogs?

FRANK: That is funny.

KELLER: Here's another one. Wanted – old dictionaries. High prices paid. Now what's a man going to do with an old dictionary?

FRANK: Why not? Probably a book collector.

KELLER: You mean he'll make a living out of that?

FRANK: Sure, there's a lot of them.

KELLER [shaking his head]: All the kind of business goin' on. In my day, either you were a lawyer, or a doctor, or you worked in a shop. Now –

FRANK: Well, I was going to be a forester once.

KELLER: Well, that shows you; in my day, there was no such thing. [Scanning the page, sweeping it with his hand] You look at a page like this you realize how ignorant you are. [Softly, with wonder, as he scans page] Psss!

FRANK [noticing tree]: Hey, what happened to your tree?

KELLER: Ain't that awful? The wind must've got it last night. You heard the wind, didn't you?

FRANK: Yeah, I got a mess in my yard, too. [Goes to tree.] What a pity. [Turning to KELLER] What'd Kate say?

KELLER: They're all asleep yet. I'm just waiting for her to see it.

FRANK [struck]: You know? – it's funny.

KELLER: What?

FRANK: Larry was born in August. He'd been twenty-seven this month. And this tree blows down.

KELLER [touched]: I'm surprised you remember his birthday, Frank. That's nice.

FRANK: Well, I'm working on his horoscope.

KELLER: How can you make him a horoscope? That's for the future, ain't it?

FRANK: Well, what I'm doing is this, see. Larry was reported missing on November twenty-fifth, right?

KELLER: Yeah?

FRANK: Well, then, we assume that if he was killed it was on November twenty-fifth. Now, what Kate wants –

KELLER: Oh, Kate asked you to make a horoscope?

FRANK: Yeah, what she wants to find out is whether November twenty-fifth was a favourable day for Larry.

KELLER: What is that, favourable day?

FRANK: Well, a favourable day for a person is a fortunate day, according to his stars. In other words it would be practically impossible for him to have died on his favourable day.

KELLER: Well, was that his favourable day? – November twenty-fifth?

FRANK: That's what I'm working on to find out. It takes time! See, the point is, if November twenty-fifth was his favourable day, then it's completely possible he's alive somewhere, because – I mean it's possible. [He notices JIM now. JIM is looking at him as though at an idiot. To JIM – with an uncertain laugh] I didn't even see you.

KELLER [to JIM]: Is he talkin' sense?

JIM: Him? He's all right. He's just completely out of his mind, that's all.

FRANK [peeved]: The trouble with you is, you don't believe in anything.

JIM: And your trouble is that you believe in anything. You didn't see my kid this morning, did you?

FRANK: No.

KELLER: Imagine? He walked off with his thermometer. Right out of his bag.

JIM [getting up]: What a problem. One look at a girl and he takes her temperature. [Goes to driveway, looks upstage towards street.]

FRANK: That boy's going to be a real doctor; he's smart.

JIM: Over my dead body he'll be a doctor. A good beginning, too.

FRANK: Why? It's an honourable profession.

JIM [*looking at him tiredly*]: Frank, will you stop talking like a civics book? [KELLER *laughs.*]

FRANK: Why, I saw a movie a couple of weeks ago, reminded me of you. There was a doctor in that picture –

KELLER: Don Ameche!

FRANK: I think it was, yeah. And he worked in his basement discovering things. That's what you ought to do; you could help humanity, instead of –

JIM: I would love to help humanity on a Warner Brothers salary.

KELLER [*pointing at him, laughing*]: That's very good, Jim.

JIM [*looking towards house*]: Well, where's the beautiful girl was supposed to be here?

FRANK [*excited*]: Annie came?

KELLER: Sure, sleepin' upstairs. We picked her up on the one o'clock train last night. Wonderful thing. Girl leaves here, a scrawny kid. Couple of years go by, she's a regular woman. Hardly recognized her, and she was running in and out of this yard all her life. That was a very happy family used to live in your house, Jim.

JIM: Like to meet her. The block can use a pretty girl. In the whole neighbourhood there's not a damned thing to look at. [SUE, JIM's *wife, enters. She is rounding forty, an overweight woman who fears it. On seeing her* JIM *wryly adds*] Except my wife, of course.

SUE [*in same spirit*]: Mrs Adams is on the phone, you dog.

JIM [*to* KELLER]: Such is the condition which prevails – [*Going to his wife*] my love, my light.

SUE: Don't sniff around me. [*Pointing to their house*] And give her a nasty answer. I can smell her perfume over the phone.

JIM: What's the matter with her now?

SUE: I don't know, dear. She sounds like she's in terrible pain
    – unless her mouth is full of candy.

JIM: Why don't you just tell her to lay down?

SUE: She enjoys it more when you tell her to lay down. And
    when are you going to see Mr Hubbard?

JIM: My dear; Mr Hubbard is not sick, and I have better
    things to do than to sit there and hold his hand.

SUE: It seems to me that for ten dollars you could hold his
    hand.

JIM [*to* KELLER]: If your son wants to play golf tell him I'm
    ready. Or if he'd like to take a trip around the world for
    about thirty years. [*He exits.*]

KELLER: Why do you needle him? He's a doctor, women are
    supposed to call him up.

SUE: All I said was Mrs Adams is on the phone. Can I have
    some of your parsley?

KELLER: Yeah, sure. [*She goes to parsley box and pulls some
    parsley.*] You were a nurse too long, Susie. You're too ...
    too ... realistic.

SUE [*laughing, pointing at him*]: Now you said it!
        [LYDIA LUBEY *enters. She is a robust, laughing girl of
        twenty-seven.*]

LYDIA: Frank, the toaster – [*Sees the others.*] Hya.

KELLER: Hello!

LYDIA [*to* FRANK]: The toaster is off again.

FRANK: Well, plug it in, I just fixed it.

LYDIA [*kindly, but insistently*]: Please, dear, fix it back like it
    was before.

FRANK: I don't know why you can't learn to turn on a simple
    thing like a toaster! [*He exits.*]

SUE [*laughing*]: Thomas Edison.

LYDIA [*apologetically*]: He's really very handy. [*She sees
    broken tree.*] Oh, did the wind get your tree?

KELLER: Yeah, last night.

LYDIA: Oh, what a pity. Annie get in?

KELLER: She'll be down soon. Wait'll you meet her, Sue, she's a knockout.

SUE: I should've been a man. People are always introducing me to beautiful women. [*To* JOE] Tell her to come over later: I imagine she'd like to see what we did with her house. And thanks. [*She exits.*]

LYDIA: Is she still unhappy, Joe?

KELLER: Annie? I don't suppose she goes around dancing on her toes, but she seems to be over it.

LYDIA: She going to get married? Is there anybody – ?

KELLER: I suppose – say, it's a couple years already. She can't mourn a boy for ever.

LYDIA: It's so strange – Annie's here and not even married. And I've got three babies. I always thought it'd be the other way around.

KELLER: Well, that's what a war does. I had two sons, now I got one. It changed all the tallies. In my day when you had sons it was an honour. Today a doctor could make a million dollars if he could figure out a way to bring a boy into the world without a trigger finger.

LYDIA: You know, I was just reading –

[*Enter* CHRIS KELLER *from house, stands in doorway.*]

LYDIA: Hya, Chris.

[FRANK *shouts from offstage.*]

FRANK: Lydia, come in here! If you want the toaster to work don't plug in the malted mixer.

LYDIA [*embarrassed, laughing*]: Did I?

FRANK: And the next time I fix something don't tell me I'm crazy! Now come in here!

LYDIA [*to* KELLER]: I'll never hear the end of this one.

KELLER [*calling to* FRANK]: So what's the difference? Instead of toast have a malted!

LYDIA: Sh! sh! [*She exits, laughing.*]

[CHRIS *watches her off. He is thirty-two; like his father, solidly built, a listener. A man capable of immense affection and loyalty. He has a cup of coffee in one hand, part of a doughnut in the other.*]

KELLER: You want the paper?

CHRIS: That's all right, just the book section. [*He bends down and pulls out part of paper on porch floor.*]

KELLER: You're always reading the book section and you never buy a book.

CHRIS [*coming down to settee*]: I like to keep abreast of my ignorance. [*He sits on settee.*]

KELLER: What is that, every week a new book comes out?

CHRIS: Lot of new books.

KELLER: All different.

CHRIS: All different.

[KELLER *shakes his head, puts knife down on bench, takes oilstone up to the cabinet.*]

KELLER: Psss! Annie up yet?

CHRIS: Mother's giving her breakfast in the dining-room.

KELLER [*looking at broken tree*]: See what happened to the tree?

CHRIS [*without looking up*]: Yeah.

KELLER: What's Mother going to say?

[BERT *runs on from driveway. He is about eight. He jumps on stool, then on* KELLER's *back.*]

BERT: You're finally up.

KELLER [*swinging him around and putting him down*]: Ha! Bert's here! Where's Tommy? He's got his father's thermometer again.

BERT: He's taking a reading.

CHRIS: What!

BERT: But it's only oral.

KELLER: Oh, well, there's no harm in oral. So what's new this morning, Bert?

BERT: Nothin'. [*He goes to broken tree, walks around it.*]

KELLER: Then you couldn't've made a complete inspection of the block. In the beginning, when I first made you a policeman you used to come in every morning with something new. Now, nothin's ever new.

BERT: Except some kids from Thirtieth Street. They started kicking a can down the block, and I made them go away because you were sleeping.

KELLER: Now you're talkin', Bert. Now you're on the ball. First thing you know I'm liable to make you a detective.

BERT [pulling him down by the lapel and whispering in his ear]: Can I see the jail now?

KELLER: Seein' the jail ain't allowed, Bert. You know that.

BERT: Aw, I betcha there isn't even a jail. I don't see any bars on the cellar windows.

KELLER: Bert, on my word of honour there's a jail in the basement. I showed you my gun, didn't I?

BERT: But that's a hunting gun.

KELLER: That's an arresting gun!

BERT: Then why don't you ever arrest anybody? Tommy said another dirty word to Doris yesterday, and you didn't even demote him.

[KELLER chuckles and winks at CHRIS, who is enjoying all this.]

KELLER: Yeah, that's a dangerous character, that Tommy. [Beckons him closer.] What word does he say?

BERT [backing away quickly in great embarrassment]: Oh, I can't say that.

KELLER [grabbing him by the shirt and pulling him back]: Well, gimme an idea.

BERT: I can't. It's not a nice word.

KELLER: Just whisper it in my ear. I'll close my eyes. Maybe I won't even hear it.

[BERT, on tiptoe, puts his lips to KELLER's ear, then in unbearable embarrassment steps back.]

BERT: I can't, Mr. Keller.

CHRIS [*laughing*]: Don't make him do that.

KELLER: Okay, Bert. I take your word. Now go out, and keep both eyes peeled.

BERT [*interested*]: For what?

KELLER: For what! Bert, the whole neighbourhood is depending on you. A policeman don't ask questions. Now peel them eyes!

BERT [*mystified, but willing*]: Okay. [*He runs off stage back of arbour.*]

KELLER [*calling after him*]: And mum's the word, Bert.
    [BERT *stops and sticks his head through the arbour.*]

BERT: About what?

KELLER: Just in general. Be v-e-r-y careful.

BERT [*nodding in bewilderment*]: Okay. [*He exits.*]

KELLER [*laughing*]: I got all the kids crazy!

CHRIS: One of these days, they'll all come in here and beat your brains out.

KELLER: What's she going to say? Maybe we ought to tell her before she sees it.

CHRIS: She saw it.

KELLER: How could she see it? I was the first one up. She was still in bed.

CHRIS: She was out here when it broke.

KELLER: When?

CHRIS: About four this morning. [*Indicating window above them*] I heard it cracking and I woke up and looked out. She was standing right here when it cracked.

KELLER: What was she doing out here four in the morning?

CHRIS: I don't know. When it cracked she ran back into the house and cried in the kitchen.

KELLER: Did you talk to her?

CHRIS: No, I – I figured the best thing was to leave her alone.
    [*Pause.*]

KELLER [*deeply touched*]: She cried hard?

CHRIS: I could hear her right through the floor of my room.

KELLER [*after a slight pause*]: What was she doing out here at that hour? [CHRIS *silent. With an undertone of anger showing*] She's dreaming about him again. She's walking around at night.

CHRIS: I guess she is.

KELLER: She's getting just like after he died. [*Slight pause.*] What's the meaning of that?

CHRIS: I don't know the meaning of it. [*Slight pause.*] But I know one thing, Dad. We've made a terrible mistake with Mother.

KELLER: What?

CHRIS: Being dishonest with her. That kind of thing always pays off, and now it's paying off.

KELLER: What do you mean, dishonest?

CHRIS: You know Larry's not coming back and I know it. Why do we allow her to go on thinking that we believe with her?

KELLER: What do you want to do, argue with her?

CHRIS: I don't want to argue with her, but it's time she realized that nobody believes Larry is alive any more. [KELLER *simply moves away, thinking, looking at the ground.*] Why shouldn't she dream of him, walk the nights waiting for him? Do we contradict her? Do we say straight out that we have no hope any more? That we haven't had any hope for years now?

KELLER [*frightened at the thought*]: You can't say that to her.

CHRIS: We've got to say it to her.

KELLER: How're you going to prove it? Can you prove it?

CHRIS: For God's sake, three years! Nobody comes back after three years. It's insane.

KELLER: To you it is, and to me. But not to her. You can talk yourself blue in the face, but there's no body and there's no grave, so where are you?

CHRIS: Sit down, Dad. I want to talk to you.

    [KELLER *looks at him searchingly a moment.*]

KELLER: The trouble is the goddam newspapers. Every month some boy turns up from nowhere, so the next one is going to be Larry, so –

CHRIS: All right, all right, listen to me. [*Slight pause.* KELLER *sits on settee.*] You know why I asked Annie here, don't you?

KELLER [*he knows, but –*]: Why?

CHRIS: You know.

KELLER: Well, I got an idea, but – What's the story?

CHRIS: I'm going to ask her to marry me. [*Slight pause.*]

    [KELLER *nods.*]

KELLER: Well, that's only your business, Chris.

CHRIS: You know it's not only my business.

KELLER: What do you want me to do? You're old enough to know your own mind.

CHRIS [*asking, annoyed*]: Then it's all right, I'll go ahead with it?

KELLER: Well, you want to be sure Mother isn't going to –

CHRIS: Then it isn't just my business.

KELLER: I'm just sayin' –

CHRIS: Sometimes you infuriate me, you know that? Isn't it your business, too, if I tell this to Mother and she throws a fit about it? You have such a talent for ignoring things.

KELLER: I ignore what I gotta ignore. The girl is Larry's girl.

CHRIS: She's not Larry's girl.

KELLER: From Mother's point of view he is not dead and you have no right to take his girl. [*Slight pause.*] Now you can go on from there if you know where to go, but I'm tellin' you I don't know where to go. See? I don't know. Now what can I do for you?

CHRIS: I don't know why it is, but every time I reach out for something I want, I have to pull back because other people will suffer. My whole bloody life, time after time after time.

KELLER: You're a considerate fella, there's nothing wrong in that.

CHRIS: To hell with that.

KELLER: Did you ask Annie yet?

CHRIS: I wanted to get this settled first.

KELLER: How do you know she'll marry you? Maybe she feels the same way Mother does?

CHRIS: Well, if she does, then that's the end of it. From her letters I think she's forgotten him. I'll find out. And then we'll thrash it out with Mother? Right? Dad, don't avoid me.

KELLER: The trouble is, you don't see enough women. You never did.

CHRIS: So what? I'm not fast with women.

KELLER: I don't see why it has to be Annie.

CHRIS: Because it is.

KELLER: That's a good answer, but it don't answer anything. You haven't seen her since you went to war. It's five years.

CHRIS: I can't help it. I know her best. I was brought up next door to her. These years when I think of someone for my wife, I think of Annie. What do you want, a diagram?

KELLER: I don't want a diagram … I – I'm – She thinks he's coming back, Chris. You marry that girl and you're pronouncing him dead. Now what's going to happen to Mother? Do you know? I don't! [Pause.]

CHRIS: All right, then, Dad.

KELLER [thinking CHRIS has retreated]: Give it some more thought.

CHRIS: I've given it three years of thought. I'd hoped that if I waited, Mother would forget Larry and then we'd have a regular wedding and everything happy. But if that can't happen here, then I'll have to get out.

KELLER: What the hell is this?

CHRIS: I'll get out. I'll get married and live some place else. Maybe in New York.

KELLER: Are you crazy?

CHRIS: I've been a good son too long, a good sucker. I'm through with it.

KELLER: You've got a business here, what the hell is this?

CHRIS: The business! The business doesn't inspire me.

KELLER: Must you be inspired?

CHRIS: Yes. I like it an hour a day. If I have to grub for money all day long at least at evening I want it beautiful. I want a family, I want some kids, I want to build something I can give myself to. Annie is in the middle of that. Now ... where do I find it?

KELLER: You mean – [*Goes to him.*] Tell me something, you mean you'd leave the business?

CHRIS: Yes. On this I would.

KELLER [*after a pause*]: Well ... you don't want to think like that.

CHRIS: Then help me stay here.

KELLER: All right, but – but don't think like that. Because what the hell did I work for? That's only for you, Chris, the whole shootin' match is for you!

CHRIS: I know that, Dad. Just you help me stay here.

KELLER [*putting a fist up to* CHRIS's *jaw*]: But don't think that way, you hear me?

CHRIS: I am thinking that way.

KELLER [*lowering his hand*]: I don't understand you, do I?

CHRIS: No, you don't. I'm a pretty tough guy.

KELLER: Yeah. I can see that.

[MOTHER *appears on porch. She is in her early fifties, a woman of uncontrolled inspirations and an overwhelming capacity for love.*]

MOTHER: Joe?

CHRIS [*going towards porch*]: Hello, Mom.

MOTHER [*indicating house behind her; to* KELLER]: Did you take a bag from under the sink?

KELLER: Yeah, I put it in the pail.

MOTHER: Well, get it out of the pail. That's my potatoes.

[CHRIS *bursts out laughing – goes up into alley*.]

KELLER [*laughing*]: I thought it was garbage.

MOTHER: Will you do me a favour, Joe? Don't be helpful.

KELLER: I can afford another bag of potatoes.

MOTHER: Minnie scoured that pail in boiling water last night. It's cleaner than your teeth.

KELLER: And I don't understand why, after I worked forty years and I got a maid, why I have to take out the garbage.

MOTHER: If you would make up your mind that every bag in the kitchen isn't full of garbage you wouldn't be throwing out my vegetables. Last time it was the onions.

[CHRIS *comes on, hands her bag*.]

KELLER: I don't like garbage in the house.

MOTHER: Then don't eat. [*She goes into the kitchen with bag*.]

CHRIS: That settles you for today.

KELLER: Yeah, I'm in last place again. I don't know, once upon a time I used to think that when I got money again I would have a maid and my wife would take it easy. Now I got money, and I got a maid, and my wife is workin' for the maid. [*He sits in one of the chairs*.]

[MOTHER *comes out on last line. She carries a pot of string beans*.]

MOTHER: It's her day off, what are you crabbing about?

CHRIS [*to* MOTHER]: Isn't Annie finished eating?

MOTHER [*looking around preoccupiedly at yard*]: She'll be right out. [*Moves*.] That wind did some job on this place. [*Of the tree*.] So much for that, thank God.

KELLER [*indicating chair beside him*]: Sit down, take it easy.

MOTHER [*pressing her hand to top of her head*]: I've got such a funny pain on the top of my head.

CHRIS: Can I get you an aspirin?

[MOTHER *picks a few petals off ground, stands there smelling them in her hand, then sprinkles them over plants.*]

MOTHER: No more roses. It's so funny ... everything decides to happen at the same time. This month is his birthday; his tree blows down, Annie comes. Everything that happened seems to be coming back. I was just down the cellar, and what do I stumble over? His baseball glove. I haven't seen it in a century.

CHRIS: Don't you think Annie looks well?

MOTHER: Fine. There's no question about it. She's a beauty. ... I still don't know what brought her here. Not that I'm not glad to see her, but –

CHRIS: I just thought we'd all like to see each other again. [MOTHER *just looks at him, nodding ever so slightly – almost as though admitting something.*] And I wanted to see her myself.

MOTHER [*as her nods halt, to* KELLER]: The only thing is I think her nose got longer. But I'll always love that girl. She's one that didn't jump into bed with somebody else as soon as it happened with her fella.

KELLER [*as though that were impossible for Annie*]: Oh, what're you – ?

MOTHER: Never mind. Most of them didn't wait till the telegrams were opened. I'm just glad she came, so you can see I'm not *completely* out of my mind. [*Sits, and rapidly breaks string beans in the pot.*]

CHRIS: Just because she isn't married doesn't mean she's been mourning Larry.

MOTHER [*with an undercurrent of observation*]: Why then isn't she?

CHRIS [*a little flustered*]: Well ... it could've been any number of things.

MOTHER [*directly at him*]: Like what, for instance?

CHRIS [*embarrassed, but standing his ground*]: I don't know. Whatever it is. Can I get you an aspirin?

[MOTHER *puts her hand to her head. She gets up and goes aimlessly towards the trees on rising.*]

MOTHER: It's not like a headache.

KELLER: You don't sleep, that's why. She's wearing out more bedroom slippers than shoes.

MOTHER: I had a terrible night. [*She stops moving.*] I never had a night like that.

CHRIS [*looking at* KELLER]: What was it, Mom? Did you dream?

MOTHER: More, more than a dream.

CHRIS [*hesitantly*]: About Larry?

MOTHER: I was fast asleep, and – [*Raising her arm over the audience.*] Remember the way he used to fly low past the house when he was in training? When we used to see his face in the cockpit going by? That's the way I saw him. Only high up. Way, way up, where the clouds are. He was so real I could reach out and touch him. And suddenly he started to fall. And crying, crying to me ... Mom, Mom! I could hear him like he was in the room. Mom! ... it was his voice! If I could touch him I knew I could stop him, if I could only – [*Breaks off, allowing her outstretched hand to fall.*] I woke up and it was so funny – The wind ... it was like the roaring of his engine. I came out here ... I must've still been half asleep. I could hear that roaring like he was going by. The tree snapped right in front of me – and I like – came awake. [*She is looking at tree. She suddenly realizes something, turns with a reprimanding finger shaking slightly at* KELLER.] See? We should never have planted that tree. I said so in the first place; it was too soon to plant a tree for him.

CHRIS [*alarmed*]: Too soon!

MOTHER [*angering*]: We rushed into it. Everybody was in such a hurry to bury him. I *said* not to plant it yet. [*To* KELLER] I *told* you to – !

CHRIS: Mother, Mother! [*She looks into his face.*] The wind blew it down. What significance has that got? What are you talking about? Mother, please ... don't go through it all again, will you? It's no good, it doesn't accomplish anything. I've been thinking, y'know? – maybe we ought to put our minds to forgetting him?

MOTHER: That's the third time you've said that this week.

CHRIS: Because it's not right; we never took up our lives again. We're like at a railroad station waiting for a train that never comes in.

MOTHER [*pressing top of her head*]: Get me an aspirin, heh?

CHRIS: Sure, and let's break out of this, heh, Mom? I thought the four of us might go out to dinner a couple of nights, maybe go dancing out at the shore.

MOTHER: Fine. [*To* KELLER] We can do it tonight.

KELLER: Swell with me!

CHRIS: Sure, let's have some fun. [*To* MOTHER] You'll start with this aspirin. [*He goes up and into house with new spirit. Her smile vanishes.*]

MOTHER [*with an accusing undertone*]: Why did he invite her here?

KELLER: Why does that bother you?

MOTHER: She's been in New York three and a half years, why all of a sudden – ?

KELLER: Well, maybe – maybe he just wanted to see her.

MOTHER: Nobody comes seven hundred miles 'just to see'.

KELLER: What do you mean? He lived next door to the girl all his life, why shouldn't he want to see her again? [MOTHER *looks at him critically*.] Don't look at me like that, he didn't tell me any more than he told you.

MOTHER [*– a warning and a question*]: He's not going to marry her.

KELLER: How do you know he's even thinking of it?

MOTHER: It's got that about it.

KELLER [*sharply watching her reaction*]: Well? So what?

MOTHER [*alarmed*]: What's going on here, Joe?

KELLER: Now listen, kid –

MOTHER [*avoiding contact with him*]: She's not his girl, Joe; she knows she's not.

KELLER: You can't read her mind.

MOTHER: Then why is she still single? New York is full of men, why isn't she married? [*Pause.*] Probably a hundred people told her she's foolish, but she's waited.

KELLER: How do you know why she waited?

MOTHER: She knows what I know, that's why. She's faithful as a rock. In my worst moments, I think of her waiting, and I know again that I'm right.

KELLER: Look, it's a nice day. What are we arguing for?

MOTHER [*warningly*]: Nobody in this house dast take her faith away, Joe. Strangers might. But not his father, not his brother.

KELLER [*exasperated*]: What do you want me to do? What do you want?

MOTHER: I want you to act like he's coming back. Both of you. Don't think I haven't noticed you since Chris invited her. I won't stand for any nonsense.

KELLER: But, Kate –

MOTHER: Because if he's not coming back, then I'll kill myself! Laugh. Laugh at me. [*She points to tree.*] But why did that happen the very night she came back? Laugh, but there are meanings in such things. She goes to sleep in his room and his memorial breaks in pieces. Look at it; look. [*She sits on bench.*] Joe –

KELLER: Calm yourself.

MOTHER: Believe with me, Joe. I can't stand all alone.

KELLER: Calm yourself.

MOTHER: Only last week a man turned up in Detroit, missing longer than Larry. You read it yourself.

KELLER: All right, all right, calm yourself.

MOTHER: You above all have got to believe, you –

KELLER [*rising*]: Why me above all?

MOTHER: Just don't stop believing.

KELLER: What does that mean, me above all?

[BERT *comes rushing on.*]

BERT: Mr Keller! Say, Mr Keller … [*Pointing up driveway*] Tommy just said it again!

KELLER [*not remembering any of it*]: Said what? Who?

BERT: The dirty word.

KELLER: Oh. Well –

BERT: Gee, aren't you going to arrest him? I warned him.

MOTHER [*with suddenness*]: Stop that, Bert. Go home. [BERT *backs up, as she advances.*] There's no jail here.

KELLER [*as though to say, 'Oh-what-the-hell-let-him-believe-there-is'*]: Kate –

MOTHER [*turning on* KELLER *furiously*]: There's no jail here! I want you to stop that jail business! [*He turns, shamed, but peeved.*]

BERT [*past her to* KELLER]: He's right across the street.

MOTHER: Go home, Bert. [BERT *turns around and goes up driveway. She is shaken. Her speech is bitten off, extremely urgent.*] I want you to stop that, Joe. That whole jail business!

KELLER [*alarmed, therefore angered*]: Look at you, look at you shaking.

MOTHER [*trying to control herself, moving about clasping her hands*]: I can't help it.

KELLER: What have I got to hide? What the hell is the matter with you, Kate?

MOTHER: I didn't say you had anything to hide, I'm just telling you to stop it! Now stop it! [*As* ANN *and* CHRIS *appear on porch.* ANN *is twenty-six, gentle but despite herself capable of holding fast to what she knows.* CHRIS *opens door for her.*]

ANN: Hya, Joe! [*She leads off a general laugh that is not self-conscious because they know one another too well.*]

CHRIS [*bringing* ANN *down, with an outstretched, chivalrous arm*]: Take a breath of that air, kid. You never get air like that in New York.

MOTHER [*genuinely overcome with it*]: Annie, where did you get that dress!

ANN: I couldn't resist. I'm taking it right off before I ruin it. [*Swings around.*] How's that for three weeks' salary?

MOTHER [*to* KELLER]: Isn't she the most – ? [*To* ANN] It's gorgeous, simply gor –

CHRIS [*to* MOTHER]: No kidding, now, isn't she the prettiest gal you ever saw?

MOTHER [*caught short by his obvious admiration, she finds herself reaching out for the glass of water and aspirin in his hand, and –*]: You gained a little weight, didn't you, darling? [*She gulps pill and drinks.*]

ANN: It comes and goes.

KELLER: Look how nice her legs turned out!

ANN [*as she runs to fence*]: Boy, the poplars got thick, didn't they?

[KELLER *moves to settee and sits.*]

KELLER: Well, it's three years, Annie. We're gettin' old, kid.

MOTHER: How does Mom like New York? [ANN *keeps looking through trees.*]

ANN [*a little hurt*]: Why'd they take our hammock away?

KELLER: Oh, no, it broke. Couple of years ago.

MOTHER: What broke? He had one of his light lunches and flopped into it.

ANN [*laughs and turns back towards* JIM's *yard*]: Oh, excuse me!

[JIM *has come to fence and is looking over it. He is smoking a cigar. As she cries out, he comes on around on stage.*]

JIM: How do you do. [*To* CHRIS] She looks very intelligent!

CHRIS: Ann, this is Jim – Doctor Bayliss.

ANN [*shaking* JIM's *hand*]: Oh, sure, he writes a lot about you.

JIM: Don't you believe it. He likes everybody. In the battalion he was known as Mother McKeller.

ANN: I can believe it. You know – ? [*To* MOTHER] It's so strange seeing him come out of that yard. [*To* CHRIS] I guess I never grew up. It almost seems that Mom and Pop are in there now. And you and my brother doing algebra, and Larry trying to copy my homework. Gosh, those dear dead days beyond recall.

JIM: Well, I hope that doesn't mean you want me to move out?

SUE [*calling from offstage*]: Jim, come in here! Mr Hubbard is on the phone!

JIM: I told you I don't want –

SUE [*commandingly sweet*]: Please, dear! Please!

JIM [*resigned*]: All right, Susie. [*Trailing off*] All right, all right … [*To* ANN] I've only met you, Ann, but if I may offer you a piece of advice – When you marry, never – even in your mind – never count your husband's money.

SUE [*from offstage*]: Jim?

JIM: At once! [*Turns and goes off.*] At once. [*He exits.*]

MOTHER [– ANN *is looking at her. She speaks meaningfully*]: I told her to take up the guitar. It'd be a common interest for them. [*They laugh.*] Well, he loves the guitar!

[ANN, *as though to overcome* MOTHER, *becomes suddenly lively, crosses to* KELLER *on settee, sits on his lap.*]

ANN: Let's eat at the shore tonight! Raise some hell around here, like we used to before Larry went!

MOTHER [*emotionally*]: You think of him! You see? [*Triumphantly.*] She thinks of him!

ANN [*with an uncomprehending smile*]: What do you mean, Kate?

MOTHER: Nothing. Just that you – remember him, he's in your thoughts.

ANN: That's a funny thing to say; how could I help remembering him?

MOTHER [– *it is drawing to a head the wrong way for her; she starts anew. She rises and comes to* ANN]: Did you hang up your things?

ANN: Yeah ... [*To* CHRIS]: Say, you've sure gone in for clothes. I could hardly find room in the closet.

MOTHER: No, don't you remember? That's Larry's room.

ANN: You mean ... they're Larry's?

MOTHER: Didn't you recognize them?

ANN [*slowly rising, a little embarrassed*]: Well, it never occurred to me that you'd – I mean the shoes are all shined.

MOTHER: Yes, dear. [*Slight pause.* ANN *can't stop staring at her. Mother breaks it by speaking with the relish of gossip, putting her arm around* ANN *and walking with her.*] For so long I've been aching for a nice conversation with you, Annie. Tell me something.

ANN: What?

MOTHER: I don't know. Something nice.

CHRIS [*wryly*]: She means do you go out much?

MOTHER: Oh, shut up.

KELLER: And are any of them serious?

MOTHER [*laughing, sits in her chair*]: Why don't you both choke?

KELLER: Annie, you can't go into a restaurant with that woman any more. In five minutes thirty-nine strange people are sitting at the table telling her their life story.

MOTHER: If I can't ask Annie a personal question –

KELLER: Askin' is all right, but don't beat her over the head. You're beatin' her, you're beatin' her. [*They are laughing.*]
    [ANN *takes pan of beans off stool, puts them on floor under chair and sits.*]

ANN [*to* MOTHER]: Don't let them bulldoze you. Ask me anything you like. What do you want to know, Kate? Come on, let's gossip.

MOTHER [*to* CHRIS *and* KELLER]: She's the only one is got any sense. [*To* ANN] Your mother – she's not getting a divorce, heh?

ANN: No, she's calmed down about it now. I think when he gets out they'll probably live together. In New York, of course.

MOTHER: That's fine. Because your father is still – I mean he's a decent man after all is said and done.

ANN: I don't care. She can take him back if she likes.

MOTHER: And you? You [*shakes her head negatively*] go out much? [*Slight pause.*]

ANN [*delicately*]: You mean am I still waiting for him?

MOTHER: Well, no. I don't expect you to wait for him but –

ANN [*kindly*]: But that's what you mean, isn't it?

MOTHER: Well ... yes.

ANN: Well, I'm not, Kate.

MOTHER [*faintly*]: You're not?

ANN: Isn't it ridiculous? You don't really imagine he's – ?

MOTHER: I know, dear, but don't say it's ridiculous, because the papers were full of it; I don't know about New York, but there was half a page about a man missing even longer than Larry, and he turned up from Burma.

CHRIS [*coming to* ANN]: He couldn't have wanted to come home very badly, Mom.

MOTHER: Don't be so smart.

CHRIS: You can have a helluva time in Burma.

ANN [*rises and swings around in back of* CHRIS]: So I've heard.

CHRIS: Mother, I'll bet you money that you're the only woman in the country who after three years is still –

MOTHER: You're sure?

CHRIS: Yes, I am.

MOTHER: Well, if you're sure then you're sure. [*She turns her head away an instant.*] They don't say it on the radio but I'm sure that in the dark at night they're still waiting for their sons.

CHRIS: Mother, you're absolutely –

MOTHER [*waving him off*]: Don't be so damned smart! Now stop it! [*Slight pause.*] There are just a few things you *don't* know. All of you. And I'll tell you one of them, Annie. Deep, deep in your heart you're always been waiting for him.

ANN [*resolutely*]: No, Kate.

MOTHER [*with increasing demand*]: But deep in your heart, Annie!

CHRIS: She ought to know, shouldn't she?

MOTHER: Don't let them tell you what to think. Listen to your heart. Only your heart.

ANN: Why does your heart tell you he's alive?

MOTHER: Because he has to be.

ANN: But why, Kate?

MOTHER [*going to her*]: Because certain things have to be, and certain things can never be. Like the sun has to rise, it has to be. That's why there's God. Otherwise anything could happen. But there's God, so certain things can never happen. I would know, Annie – just like I knew the day he [*indicates* CHRIS] went into that terrible battle. Did he write me? Was it in the papers? No, but that morning I couldn't raise my head off the pillow. Ask Joe. Suddenly, I knew. I knew! And he was nearly killed that day. Ann, you *know* I'm right!

[ANN *stands there in silence, then turns trembling, going upstage.*]

ANN: No, Kate.

MOTHER: I have to have some tea.

[FRANK *appears, carrying ladder.*]

FRANK: Annie! [*Coming down.*] How are you, gee whiz!

ANN [*taking his hand*]: Why, Frank, you're losing your hair.

KELLER: He's got responsibility.

FRANK: Gee whiz!

KELLER: Without Frank the stars wouldn't know when to come out.

FRANK [*laughs; to* ANN]: You look more womanly. You've matured. You –

KELLER: Take it easy, Frank, you're a married man.

ANN [*as they laugh*]: You still haberdashering?

FRANK: Why not? Maybe I too can get to be president. How's your brother? Got his degree, I hear.

ANN: Oh, George has his own office now!

FRANK: Don't say! [*Funereally*] And your dad? Is he – ?

ANN [*abruptly*]: Fine. I'll be in to see Lydia.

FRANK [*sympathetically*]: How about it, does Dad expect a parole soon?

ANN [*with growing ill-ease*]: I really don't know, I –

FRANK [*staunchly defending her father for her sake*]: I mean because I feel, y'know, that if an intelligent man like your father is put in prison, there ought to be a law that says either you execute him, or let him go after a year.

CHRIS [*interrupting*]: Want a hand with that ladder, Frank?

FRANK [*taking cue*]: That's all right, I'll – [*Picks up ladder.*] I'll finish the horoscope tonight, Kate. [*Embarrassed*] See you later, Ann, you look wonderful. [*He exits. They look at* ANN.]

ANN [*to* CHRIS, *as she sits slowly on stool*]: Haven't they stopped talking about Dad?

CHRIS [*comes down and sits on arm of chair*]: Nobody talks about him any more.

KELLER [*rises and comes to her*]: Gone and forgotten, kid.

ANN: Tell me. Because I don't want to meet anybody on the block if they're going to –

CHRIS: I don't want you to worry about it.

ANN [*to* KELLER]: Do they still remember the case, Joe? Do they talk about you?

KELLER: The only one still talks about it is my wife.

MOTHER: That's because you keep on playing policemen with the kids. All their parents hear out of you is jail, jail, jail.

KELLER: Actually what happened was that when I got home from the penitentiary the kids got very interested in me. You know kids. I was [*laughs*] like the expert on the jail situation. And as time passed they got it confused and ... I ended up a detective. [*Laughs.*]

MOTHER: Except that *they* didn't get it confused. [*To* ANN] He hands out police badges from the Post Toasties boxes. [*They laugh.*]

   [ANN *rises and comes to* KELLER, *putting her arm around his shoulder.*]

ANN [*wondrously at them, happy*]: Gosh, it's wonderful to hear you laughing about it.

CHRIS: Why, what'd you expect?

ANN: The last thing I remember on this block was one word – 'Murderers!' Remember that, Kate? – Mrs Hammond standing in front of our house and yelling that word? She's still around, I suppose?

MOTHER: They're all still around.

KELLER: Don't listen to her. Every Saturday night the whole gang is playin' poker in this arbour. All the ones who yelled murderer takin' my money now.

MOTHER: Don't, Joe; she's a sensitive girl, don't fool her. [*To* ANN] They still remember about Dad. It's different with him. [*Indicates* JOE.] He was exonerated, your father's still there. That's why I wasn't so enthusiastic about your coming. Honestly, I know how sensitive you are, and I told Chris, I said –

KELLER: Listen, you do like I did and you'll be all right. The day I come home, I got out of my car – but not in front of the house ... on the corner. You should've been here, Annie, and you too, Chris; you'd-a-seen something. Everybody knew I was getting out that day; the porches were loaded. Picture it now; none of them believed I was innocent. The story was, I pulled a fast one getting myself exonerated. So I get out of my car, and I walk down the street. But very slow. And with a smile. The beast! I was the beast; the guy who sold cracked cylinder heads to the Army Air Force; the guy who made twenty-one P-40s crash in Australia. Kid, walkin' down the street that day I was guilty as hell. Except I wasn't, and there was a court paper in my pocket to prove I wasn't, and I walked ... past ... the porches. Result? Fourteen months later I had one of the best shops in the state again, a respected man again; bigger than ever.

CHRIS [*with admiration*]: Joe McGuts.

KELLER [*now with great force*]: That's the only way you lick 'em is guts! [*To* ANN] The worst thing you did was to move away from here. You made it tough for your father when he gets out. That's why I tell you, I like to see him move back right on this block.

MOTHER [*pained*]: How could they move back?

KELLER: It ain't gonna end *till* they move back! [*To* ANN] Till people play cards with him again, and talk with him, and smile with him – you play cards with a man you know he can't be a murderer. And the next time you write him I like you to tell him just what I said. [ANN *simply stares at him.*] You hear me?

ANN [*surprised*]: Don't you hold anything against him?

KELLER: Annie, I never believed in crucifying people.

ANN [*mystified*]: But he was your partner, he dragged you through the mud.

KELLER: Well, he ain't my sweetheart, but you gotta forgive, don't you?

ANN: You either, Kate? Don't you feel any – ?

KELLER [*to* ANN]: The next time you write Dad –

ANN: I don't write him.

KELLER [*struck*]: Well, every now and then you –

ANN [*a little shamed, but determined*]: No, I've *never* written to him. Neither has my brother. [*To* CHRIS] Say, do you feel this way, too?

CHRIS: He murdered twenty-one pilots.

KELLER: What the hell kinda talk is that?

MOTHER: That's not a thing to say about a man.

ANN: What else can you say? When they took him away I followed him, went to him every visiting-day. I was crying all the time. Until the news came about Larry. Then I realized. It's wrong to pity a man like that. Father or no father, there's only one way to look at him. He knowingly shipped out parts that would crash an airplane. And how do you know Larry wasn't one of them?

MOTHER: I was waiting for that. [*Going to her*] As long as you're here, Annie, I want to ask you never to say that again.

ANN: You surprise me. I thought you'd be mad at him.

MOTHER: What your father did had nothing to do with Larry. Nothing.

ANN: But we can't know that.

MOTHER [*striving for control*]: As long as you're here!

ANN [*perplexed*]: But, Kate –

MOTHER: Put that out of your head!

KELLER: Because –

MOTHER [*quickly to* KELLER]: That's all, that's enough. [*Places her hand on her head.*] Come inside now, and have some tea with me. [*She turns and goes up steps.*]

KELLER [*to* ANN]: The one thing you –

MOTHER [*sharply*]: He's not dead, so there's no argument! Now come!

KELLER [*angrily*]: In a minute! [MOTHER *turns and goes into house.*] Now look, Annie –

CHRIS: All right, Dad, forget it.

KELLER: No, she dasn't feel that way. Annie –

CHRIS: I'm sick of the whole subject, now cut it out.

KELLER: You want her to go on like this? [*To* ANN] Those cylinder heads went into P-40s only. What's the matter with you? You know Larry never flew a P-40.

CHRIS: So who flew those P-40s, pigs?

KELLER: The man was a fool, but don't make a murderer out of him. You got no sense? Look what it does to her! [*To* ANN] Listen, you gotta appreciate what was doin' in that shop in the war. The both of you! It was a madhouse. Every half hour the Major callin' for cylinder heads, they were whippin' us with the telephone. The trucks were hauling them away hot, damn near. I mean just try to see it human, see it human. All of a sudden a batch comes out with a crack. That happens, that's the business. A fine, hairline crack. All right, so – so he's a little man, your father, always scared of loud voices. What'll the Major say? – Half a day's production shot. ... What'll I say? You know what I mean? Human. [*He pauses.*] So he takes out his tools and he – covers over the cracks. All right – that's bad, it's wrong, but that's what a little man does. If I could have gone in that day I'd-a told him – junk 'em, Steve, we can afford it. But alone he was afraid. But I know he meant no harm. He believed they'd hold up a hundred per cent. That's a mistake, but it ain't murder. You mustn't feel that way about him. You understand me? It ain't right.

ANN [*she regards him a moment*]: Joe, let's forget it.

KELLER: Annie, the day the news came about Larry he was in the next cell to mine – Dad. And he cried, Annie – he cried half the night.

ANN [*touched*]: He shoulda cried all night. [*Slight pause.*]

KELLER [*almost angered*]: Annie, I do not understand why you – ?

CHRIS [*breaking in – with nervous urgency*]: Are you going to stop it?

ANN: Don't yell at him. He just wants everybody happy.

KELLER [*clasps her around waist, smiling*]: That's my sentiments. Can you stand steak?

CHRIS: And champagne!

KELLER: Now you're operatin'! I'll call Swanson's for a table! Big time tonight, Annie!

ANN: Can't scare me.

KELLER [*to* CHRIS, *pointing at* ANN]: I like that girl. Wrap her up. [*They laugh. Goes up porch.*] You got nice legs, Annie! ... I want to see everybody drunk tonight. [*Pointing to* CHRIS] Look at him, he's blushin'! [*He exits, laughing, into house.*]

CHRIS [*calling after him*]: Drink your tea, Casanova. [*He turns to* ANN.] Isn't he a great guy?

ANN: You're the only one I know who loves his parents.

CHRIS: I know. It went out of style, didn't it?

ANN [*with a sudden touch of sadness*]: It's all right. It's a good thing. [*She looks about.*] You know? It's lovely here. The air is sweet.

CHRIS [*hopefully*]: You're not sorry you came?

ANN: Not sorry, no. But I'm – not going to stay.

CHRIS: Why?

ANN: In the first place, your mother as much as told me to go.

CHRIS: Well –

ANN: You saw that – and then you – you've been kind of –

CHRIS: What?

ANN: Well ... kind of embarrassed ever since I got here.

CHRIS: The trouble is I planned on kind of sneaking up on you over a period of a week or so. But they take it for granted that we're all set.

ANN: I knew they would. Your mother anyway.

CHRIS: How did you know?

ANN: From *her* point of view, why else would I come?

CHRIS: Well ... would you want to? [ANN *still studies him.*] I guess you know this is why I asked you to come.

ANN: I guess this is why I came.

CHRIS: Ann, I love you. I love you a great deal. [*Finally*] I love you. [*Pause. She waits.*] I have no imagination ... that's all I know to tell you. [ANN *is waiting, ready.*] I'm embarrassing you. I didn't want to tell it to you here. I wanted some place we'd never been; a place where we'd be brand new to each other. ... You feel it's wrong here, don't you? This yard, this chair? I want you to be ready for me. I don't want to win you away from anything.

ANN [*putting her arms around him*]: Oh, Chris, I've been ready a long, long time!

CHRIS: Then he's gone for ever. You're sure.

ANN: I almost got married two years ago.

CHRIS: Why didn't you?

ANN: You started to write to me – [*Slight pause.*]

CHRIS: You felt something that far back?

ANN: Every day since!

CHRIS: Ann, why didn't you let me know?

ANN: I was waiting for you, Chris. Till then you never wrote. And when you did, what did you say? You sure can be ambiguous, you know.

CHRIS [*looks towards house, then at her, trembling*]: Give me a kiss, Ann. Give me a – [*They kiss.*] God, I kissed you, Annie, I kissed Annie. How long, how long I've been waiting to kiss you!

ANN: I'll never forgive you. Why did you wait all these years? All I've done is sit and wonder if I was crazy for thinking of you.

CHRIS: Annie, we're going to live now! I'm going to make

you so happy. [*He kisses her, but without their bodies touching.*]

ANN [*a little embarrassed*]: Not like that you're not.

CHRIS: I kissed you. ...

ANN: Like Larry's brother. Do it like you, Chris. [*He breaks away from her abruptly.*] What is it, Chris?

CHRIS: Let's drive some place ... I want to be alone with you.

ANN: No ... what is it, Chris, your mother?

CHRIS: No – nothing like that.

ANN: Then what's wrong? Even in your letters, there was something ashamed.

CHRIS: Yes. I suppose I have been. But it's going from me.

ANN: You've got to tell me –

CHRIS: I don't know how to start. [*He takes her hand.*]

ANN: It wouldn't work this way. [*Slight pause.*]

CHRIS [*speaks quietly, factually at first*]: It's all mixed up with so many other things. ... You remember, overseas, I was in command of a company?

ANN: Yeah, sure.

CHRIS: Well, I lost them.

ANN: How many?

CHRIS: Just about all.

ANN: Oh, gee!

CHRIS: It takes a little time to toss that off. Because they weren't just men. For instance, one time it'd been raining several days and this kid came to me, and gave me his last pair of dry socks. Put them in my pocket. That's only a little thing – but ... that's the kind of guys I had. They didn't die; they killed themselves for each other. I mean that exactly; a little more selfish and they'd 've been here today. And I got an idea – watching them go down. Everything was being destroyed, see, but it seemed to me that one new thing was made. A kind of – responsibility. Man for man. You understand me? – To show that, to bring that on to the earth again like some kind of a monument and everyone would feel it standing there, behind him, and it would make a difference to him. [*Pause.*] And then I came home and it was incredible. I – there was no meaning in it here; the whole thing to them was a kind of a – bus accident. I went to work with Dad, and that rat-race again. I felt – what you said – ashamed somehow. Because nobody was changed at all. It seemed to make suckers out of a lot of guys. I felt wrong to be alive, to open the bank-book, to drive the new car, to see the new refrigerator. I mean you can take those things out of a war, but when you drive that car you've got to know that it came out of the love a man can have for a man, you've got to be a little better because of that. Otherwise what you have is really loot, and there's blood on it. I didn't want to take any of it. And I guess that included you.

ANN: And you still feel that way?

CHRIS: I want you now, Annie.

ANN: Because you mustn't feel that way any more. Because you have a right to whatever you have. Everything, Chris, understand that? To me, too ... And the money, there's nothing wrong in your money. Your father put hundreds of planes in the air, you should be proud. A man should be paid for that. ...

CHRIS: Oh Annie, Annie ... I'm going to make a fortune for you!

KELLER [*offstage*]: Hello ... Yes. Sure.

ANN [*laughing softly*]: What'll I do with a fortune?
    [*They kiss.* KELLER *enters from house.*]

KELLER [*thumbing towards house*]: Hey, Ann, your brother –
    [*They step apart shyly* KELLER *comes down, and wryly*]
    What is this, Labour Day?

CHRIS [*waving him away, knowing the kidding will be endless*]:
    All right, all right.

ANN: You shouldn't burst out like that.

KELLER: Well, nobody told me it was Labour Day. [*Looks around.*] Where's the hot dogs?

CHRIS [*loving it*]: All right. You said it once.

KELLER: Well, as long as I know it's Labour Day from now on, I'll wear a bell around my neck.

ANN [*affectionately*]: He's so subtle!

CHRIS: George Bernard Shaw as an elephant.

KELLER: George – hey, you kissed it out of my head – your brother's on the phone.

ANN [*surprised*]: My brother?

KELLER: Yeah, George. Long distance.

ANN: What's the matter, is anything wrong?

KELLER: I don't know, Kate's talking to him. Hurry up, she'll cost him five dollars.

ANN [*takes a step upstage, then comes down towards* CHRIS]: I wonder if we ought to tell your mother yet? I mean I'm not very good in an argument.

CHRIS: We'll wait till tonight. After dinner. Now don't get tense, just leave it to me.

KELLER: What're you telling her?

CHRIS: Go ahead, Ann. [*With misgivings,* ANN *goes up and into house.*] We're getting married, Dad. [KELLER *nods indecisively.*] Well, don't you say anything?

KELLER [*distracted*]: I'm glad, Chris, I'm just – George is calling from Columbus.

CHRIS: Columbus!

KELLER: Did Annie tell you he was going to see his father today?

CHRIS: No, I don't think she knew anything about it.

KELLER [*asking uncomfortably*]: Chris! You – you think you know her pretty good?

CHRIS [*hurt and apprehensive*]: What kind of a question?

KELLER: I'm just wondering. All these years George don't go

to see his father. Suddenly he goes ... and she comes here.

CHRIS: Well, what about it?

KELLER: It's crazy, but it comes to my mind. She don't hold nothin' against me, does she?

CHRIS [angry]: I don't know what you're talking about.

KELLER [a little more combatively]: I'm just talkin'. To his last day in court the man blamed it all on me; and this is his daughter. I mean if she was sent here to find out something?

CHRIS [angered]: Why? What is there to find out?

ANN [on phone, offstage]: Why are you so excited, George? What happened there?

KELLER: I mean if they want to open up the case again, for the nuisance value, to hurt us?

CHRIS: Dad ... how could you think that of her?

ANN [still on phone]: But what did he say to you, for God's sake? } Together

KELLER: It couldn't be, heh. You know.

CHRIS: Dad, you amaze me ...

KELLER [breaking in]: All right, forget it, forget it. [With great force, moving about] I want a clean start for you, Chris. I want a new sign over the plant – Christopher Keller, Incorporated.

CHRIS [a little uneasily]: J. O. Keller is good enough.

KELLER: We'll talk about it. I'm going to build you a house, stone, with a driveway from the road. I want you to spread out, Chris, I want you to use what I made for you. [He is close to him now.] I mean, with joy, Chris, without shame ... with joy.

CHRIS [touched]: I will, Dad.

KELLER [with deep emotion]: Say it to me.

CHRIS: Why?

KELLER: Because sometimes I think you're ... ashamed of the money.

CHRIS: No, don't feel that.

KELLER: Because it's good money, there's nothing wrong with that money.

CHRIS [*a little frightened*]: Dad, you don't have to tell me this.

KELLER [– *with overriding affection and self-confidence now. He grips* CHRIS *by the back of the neck, and with laughter between his determined jaws*]: Look, Chris, I'll go to work on Mother for you. We'll get her so drunk tonight we'll all get married! [*Steps away, with a wide gesture of his arm.*] There's gonna be a wedding, kid, like there never was seen! Champagne, tuxedos – !

[*He breaks off as* ANN's *voice comes out loud from the house where she is still talking on phone.*]

ANN: Simply because when you get excited you don't control yourself. ... [MOTHER *comes out of house.*] Well, what did he tell you for God's sake? [*Pause.*] All right, come then. [*Pause.*] Yes, they'll all be here. Nobody's running away from you. And try to get hold of yourself, will you? [*Pause.*] All right, all right. Good-bye. [*There is a brief pause as* ANN *hangs up receiver, then comes out of kitchen.*]

CHRIS: Something happen?

KELLER: He's coming here?

ANN: On the seven o'clock. He's in Columbus. [*To* MOTHER] I told him it would be all right.

KELLER: Sure, fine! Your father took sick?

ANN [*mystified*]: No, George didn't say he was sick. I – [*shaking it off*] I don't know, I suppose it's something stupid, you know my brother – [*She comes to* CHRIS.] Let's go for a drive, or something ...

CHRIS: Sure. Give me the keys, Dad.

MOTHER: Drive through the park. It's beautiful now.

CHRIS: Come on, Ann. [*To them*] Be back right away.

ANN [*as she and* CHRIS *exit up driveway*]: See you.

[MOTHER *comes down towards* KELLER, *her eyes fixed on him.*]

KELLER: Take your time. [*To* MOTHER] What does George want?

MOTHER: He's been in Columbus since this morning with Steve. He's gotta see Annie right away, he says.

KELLER: What for?

MOTHER: I don't know. [*She speaks with warning.*] He's a lawyer now, Joe. George is a lawyer. All these years he never even sent a postcard to Steve. Since he got back from the war, not a postcard.

KELLER: So what?

MOTHER [*her tension breaking out*]: Suddenly he takes an airplane from New York to see him. An airplane!

KELLER: Well? So?

MOTHER [*trembling*]: Why?

KELLER: I don't read minds. Do you?

MOTHER: Why, Joe? What has Steve suddenly got to tell him that he takes an airplane to see him?

KELLER: What do I care what Steve's got to tell him?

MOTHER: You're sure, Joe?

KELLER [*frightened, but angry*]: Yes, I'm sure.

MOTHER [*sits stiffly in a chair*]: Be smart now, Joe. The boy is coming. Be smart.

KELLER [*desperately*]: Once and for all, did you hear what I said? I said I'm sure!

MOTHER [*nods weakly*]: All right, Joe. [*He straightens up.*] Just ... be smart.

[KELLER, *in hopeless fury, looks at her, turns around, goes up to porch and into house, slamming screen door violently behind him.* MOTHER *sits in chair downstage, stiffly, staring, seeing.*]

CURTAIN

ACT TWO

[*As twilight falls, that evening. On the rise,* CHRIS *is discovered sawing the broken-off tree, leaving stump standing alone. He is dressed in good pants, white shoes, but without a shirt. He disappears with tree up the alley when* MOTHER *appears on porch. She comes down and stands watching him. She has on a dressing-gown, carries a tray of grape-juice drink in a pitcher, and glasses with sprigs of mint in them.*]

MOTHER [*calling up alley*]: Did you have to put on good pants to do that? [*She comes downstage and puts tray on table in the arbour. Then looks around uneasily, then feels pitcher for coolness.* CHRIS *enters from alley brushing off his hands.*] You notice there's more light with that thing gone?

CHRIS: Why aren't you dressing?

MOTHER: It's suffocating upstairs. I made a grape drink for Georgie. He always liked grape. Come and have some.

CHRIS [*impatiently*]: Well, come on, get dressed. And what's Dad sleeping so much for? [*He goes to table and pours a glass of juice.*]

MOTHER: He's worried. When he's worried he sleeps. [*Pauses. Looks into his eyes.*] We're dumb, Chris. Dad and I are stupid people. We don't know anything. You've got to protect us.

CHRIS: You're silly; what's there to be afraid of?

MOTHER: To his last day in court Steve never gave up the idea that Dad made him do it. If they're going to open the case again I won't live through it.

CHRIS: George is just a damn fool, Mother. How can you take him seriously?

MOTHER: That family hates us. Maybe even Annie –

CHRIS: Oh, now, Mother ...

MOTHER: You think just because you like everybody, they like you!

CHRIS: All right, stop working yourself up. Just leave everything to me.

MOTHER: When George goes home tell her to go with him.

CHRIS [*non-committally*]: Don't worry about Annie.

MOTHER: Steve is her father, too.

CHRIS: Are you going to cut it out? Now, come.

MOTHER [*going upstage with him*]: You don't realize how people can hate, Chris, they can hate so much they'll tear the world to pieces.

[ANN, *dressed up, appears on porch.*]

CHRIS: Look! She's dressed already. [*As he and* MOTHER *mount porch.*] I've just got to put on a shirt.

ANN [*in a preoccupied way*]: Are you feeling well, Kate?

MOTHER: What's the difference, dear. There are certain people, y'know, the sicker they get the longer they live. [*She goes into house.*]

CHRIS: You look nice.

ANN: We're going to tell her tonight.

CHRIS: Absolutely, don't worry about it.

ANN: I wish we could tell her now. I can't stand scheming. My stomach gets hard.

CHRIS: It's not scheming, we'll just get her in a better mood.

MOTHER [*offstage, in the house*]: Joe, are you going to sleep all day!

ANN [*laughing*]: The only one who's relaxed is your father. He's fast asleep.

CHRIS: I'm relaxed.

ANN: Are you?

CHRIS: Look. [*He holds out his hand and makes it shake.*] Let me know when George gets here.

[*He goes into the house.* ANN *moves aimlessly, and then is drawn towards the tree stump. She goes to it, hesitantly touches broken top in the hush of her thoughts. Offstage* LYDIA *calls,* 'Johnny! Come get your supper!' SUE *enters, and halts, seeing* ANN.]

SUE: Is my husband – ?

ANN [*turns, startled*]: Oh!

SUE: I'm terribly sorry.

ANN: It's all right, I – I'm a little silly about the dark.

SUE [*looks about*]: It is getting dark.

ANN: Are you looking for your husband?

SUE: As usual. [*Laughs tiredly.*] He spends so much time here, they'll be charging him rent.

ANN: Nobody was dressed so he drove over to the depot to pick up my brother.

SUE: Oh, your brother's in?

ANN: Yeah, they ought to be here any minute now. Will you have a cold drink?

SUE: I will, thanks. [ANN *goes to table and pours.*] My husband. Too hot to drive me to beach. Men are like little boys; for the neighbours they'll always cut the grass.

ANN: People like to do things for the Kellers. Been that way since I can remember.

SUE: It's amazing. I guess your brother's coming to give you away, heh?

ANN [*giving her drink*]: I don't know. I suppose.

SUE: You must be all nerved up.

ANN: It's always a problem getting yourself married, isn't it?

SUE: That depends on your shape, of course. I don't see why you should have had a problem.

ANN: I've had chances –

SUE: I'll bet. It's romantic ... it's very unusual to me, marrying the brother of your sweetheart.

ANN: I don't know. I think it's mostly that whenever I need

somebody to tell me the truth I've always thought of Chris. When he tells you something you know it's so. He relaxes me.

SUE: And he's got money. That's important, you know.

ANN: It wouldn't matter to me.

SUE: You'd be surprised. It makes all the difference. I married an intern. On my salary. And that was bad, because as soon as a woman supports a man he owes her something. You can never owe somebody without resenting them. [ANN *laughs*.] That's true, you know.

ANN: Underneath, I think the doctor is very devoted.

SUE: Oh, certainly. But it's bad when a man always sees the bars in front of him. Jim thinks he's in jail all the time.

ANN: Oh ...

SUE: That's why I've been intending to ask you a small favour, Ann. It's something very important to me.

ANN: Certainly, if I can do it.

SUE: You can. When you take up housekeeping, try to find a place away from here.

ANN: Are you fooling?

SUE: I'm very serious. My husband is unhappy with Chris around.

ANN: How is that?

SUE: Jim's a successful doctor. But he's got an idea he'd like to do medical research. Discover things. You see?

ANN: Well, isn't that good?

SUE: Research pays twenty-five dollars a week minus laundering the hair-shirt. You've got to give up your life to go into it.

ANN: How does Chris –

SUE [*with growing feeling*]: Chris makes people want to be better than it's possible to be. He does that to people.

ANN: Is that bad?

SUE: My husband has a family, dear. Every time he has a

session with Chris he feels as though he's compromising by not giving up everything for research. As though Chris or anybody else isn't compromising. It happens with Jim every couple of years. He meets a man and makes a statue out of him.

ANN: Maybe he's right. I don't mean that Chris is a statue, but –

SUE: Now darling, you know he's not right.

ANN: I don't agree with you. Chris –

SUE: Let's face it, dear. Chris is working with his father, isn't he? He's taking money out of that business every week in the year.

ANN: What of it?

SUE: You ask me what of it?

ANN: I certainly do. [*She seems about to burst out.*] You oughtn't cast aspersions like that, I'm surprised at you.

SUE: You're surprised at me!

ANN: He'd never take five cents out of that plant if there was anything wrong with it.

SUE: You know that.

ANN: I know it. I resent everything you've said.

SUE [*moving towards her*]: You know what I resent, dear?

ANN: Please, I don't want to argue.

SUE: I resent living next door to the Holy Family. It makes me look like a bum, you understand?

ANN: I can't do anything about that.

SUE: Who is he to ruin a man's life? Everybody knows Joe pulled a fast one to get out of jail.

ANN: That's not true!

SUE: Then why don't you go out and talk to people? Go on, talk to them. There's not a person on the block who doesn't know the truth.

ANN: That's a lie. People come here all the time for cards and –

SUE: So what? They give him credit for being smart. I do, too, I've got nothing against Joe. But if Chris wants people to put on the hair-shirt let him take off his broadcloth. He's driving my husband crazy with that phoney idealism of his, and I'm at the end of my rope on it! [CHRIS *enters on porch, wearing shirt and tie now. She turns quickly, hearing. With a smile*] Hello, darling. How's Mother?

CHRIS: I thought George came.

SUE: No, it was just us.

CHRIS [*coming down to them*]: Susie, do me a favour, heh? Go up to Mother and see if you can calm her. She's all worked up.

SUE: She still doesn't know about you two?

CHRIS [*laughs a little*]: Well, she senses it, I guess. You know my mother.

SUE [*going up to porch*]: Oh, yeah, she's psychic.

CHRIS: Maybe there's something in the medicine chest.

SUE: I'll give her one of everything. [*On porch*] Don't worry about Kate; couple of drinks, dance her around a little ... She'll love Ann. [*To* ANN] Because you're the female version of him. [CHRIS *laughs.*] Don't be alarmed, I said version. [*She goes into house.*]

CHRIS: Interesting woman, isn't she?

ANN: Yeah, she's very interesting.

CHRIS: She's a great nurse, you know, she –

ANN [*in tension, but trying to control it*]: Are you still doing that?

CHRIS [*sensing something wrong, but still smiling*]: Doing what?

ANN: As soon as you get to know somebody you find a distinction for them. How do you know she's a great nurse?

CHRIS: What's the matter, Ann?

ANN: The woman hates you. She despises you!

CHRIS: Hey ... What's hit you?

ANN: Gee, Chris –

CHRIS: What happened here?

ANN: You never – Why didn't you tell me?

CHRIS: Tell you what?

ANN: She says they think Joe is guilty.

CHRIS: What difference does it make what they think?

ANN: I don't care what they think, I just don't understand why you took the trouble to deny it. You said it was all forgotten.

CHRIS: I didn't want you to feel there was anything wrong in you coming here, that's all. I know a lot of people think my father was guilty, and I assumed there might be some question in your mind.

ANN: But I never once said I suspected him.

CHRIS: Nobody says it.

ANN: Chris, I know how much you love him, but it could never –

CHRIS: Do you think I could forgive him if he'd done that thing?

ANN: I'm not here out of a blue sky, Chris. I turned my back on my father, if there's anything wrong here now –

CHRIS: I know that, Ann.

ANN: George is coming from Dad, and I don't think it's with a blessing.

CHRIS: He's welcome here. You've got nothing to fear from George.

ANN: Tell me that … just tell me that.

CHRIS: The man is innocent, Ann. Remember he was falsely accused once and it put him through hell. How would you behave if you were faced with the same thing again? Annie, believe me, there's nothing wrong for you here, believe me, kid.

ANN: All right, Chris, all right. [*They embrace as* KELLER *appears quietly on porch.* ANN *simply studies him.*]

KELLER: Every time I come out here it looks like Playland! [*They break and laugh in embarrassment.*]

CHRIS: I thought you were going to shave?

KELLER [*sitting on bench*]: In a minute. I just woke up, I can't see nothin'.

ANN: You look shaved.

KELLER: Oh, no. [*Massages his jaw.*] Gotta be extra special tonight. Big night, Annie. So how's it feel to be a married woman?

ANN [*laughs*]: I don't know, yet.

KELLER [*to* CHRIS]: What's the matter, you slippin'? [*He takes a little box of apples from under the bench as they talk.*]

CHRIS: The great roué!

KELLER: What is that, roué?

CHRIS: It's French.

KELLER: Don't talk dirty. [*They laugh.*]

CHRIS [*to* ANN]: You ever meet a bigger ignoramus?

KELLER: Well, somebody's got to make a living.

ANN [*as they laugh*]: That's telling him.

KELLER: I don't know, everybody's gettin' so goddam educated in this country there'll be nobody to take away the garbage. [*They laugh.*] It's gettin' so the only dumb ones left are the bosses.

ANN: You're not so dumb, Joe.

KELLER: I know, but you go into our plant, for instance. I got so many lieutenants, majors, and colonels that I'm ashamed to ask somebody to sweep the floor. I gotta be careful I'll insult somebody. No kiddin'. It's a tragedy: you stand on the street today and spit, you're gonna hit a college man.

CHRIS: Well, don't spit.

KELLER [*breaks apple in half, passing it to* ANN *and* CHRIS]: I mean to say, it's comin' to a pass. [*He takes a breath.*] I been thinkin', Annie ... your brother, George. I been thinkin' about your brother George. When he comes I like you to *brooch* something to him.

CHRIS: Broach.

KELLER: What's the matter with brooch?

CHRIS [*smiling*]: It's not English.

KELLER: When I went to night-school it was brooch.

ANN [*laughing*]: Well, in day-school it's broach.

KELLER: Don't surround me, will you? Seriously, Ann ...
You say he's not well. George, I been thinkin', why
should he knock himself out in New York with that cut-
throat competition, when I got so many friends here; I'm
very friendly with some big lawyers in town. I could set
George up here.

ANN: That's awfully nice of you, Joe.

KELLER: No, kid, it ain't nice of me. I want you to understand me. I'm thinking of Chris. [*Slight pause.*] See ... this
is what I mean. You get older, you want to feel that you –
accomplished something. My only accomplishment is my
son. I ain't brainy. That's all I accomplished. Now, a year,
eighteen months, your father'll be a free man. Who is he
going to come to, Annie? His baby. You. He'll come, old,
mad, into your house.

ANN: That can't matter any more, Joe.

KELLER: I don't want that to come between us. [*Gestures
between* CHRIS *and himself.*]

ANN: I can only tell you that that could never happen.

KELLER: You're in love now, Annie, but believe me, I'm
older than you and I know – a daughter is a daughter, and
a father is a father. And it could happen. [*He pauses.*] I like
you and George to go to him in prison and tell him ...
'Dad, Joe wants to bring you into the business when you
get out.'

ANN [*surprised, even shocked*]: You'd have him as a partner?

KELLER: No, no partner. A good job. [*Pause. He sees she is
shocked, a little mystified. He gets up, speaks more nervously.*]
I want him to know, Annie ... while he's sitting there I

want him to know that when he gets out he's got a place waitin' for him. It'll take his bitterness away. To know you got a place … it sweetens you.

ANN: Joe, you owe him nothing.

KELLER: I owe him a good kick in the teeth, but he's your father.

CHRIS: Then kick him in the teeth! I don't want him in the plant, so that's that! You understand? And besides, don't talk about him like that. People misunderstand you!

KELLER: And I don't understand why she has to crucify the man.

CHRIS: Well, it's her father, if she feels –

KELLER: No, no.

CHRIS [almost angrily]: What's it to you? Why – ?

KELLER [– a commanding outburst in high nervousness]: A father is a father! [As though the outburst had revealed him, he looks about, wanting to retract it. His hand goes to his cheek.] I better – I better shave. [He turns and a smile is on his face. To ANN] I didn't mean to yell at you, Annie.

ANN: Let's forget the whole thing, Joe.

KELLER: Right. [To CHRIS] She's likeable.

CHRIS [a little peeved at the man's stupidity]: Shave, will you?

KELLER: Right again.

[As he turns to porch LYDIA comes hurrying from her house.]

LYDIA: I forgot all about it. [Seeing CHRIS and ANN] Hya. [To JOE] I promised to fix Kate's hair for tonight. Did she comb it yet?

KELLER: Always a smile, hey, Lydia?

LYDIA: Sure, why not?

KELLER [going up on porch]: Come on up and comb my Katie's hair. [LYDIA goes up on porch.] She's got a big night, make her beautiful.

LYDIA: I will.

KELLER [holds door open for her and she goes into kitchen. To

CHRIS *and* ANN]: Hey, that could be a song. [*He sings softly.*]
 Come on up and comb my Katie's hair ...
 Oh, come on up, 'cause she's my lady fair –
[*To* ANN] How's that for one year of night-school? [*He
continues singing as he goes into kitchen.*]
 Oh, come on up, come on up, and comb my
 lady's hair –

[JIM BAYLISS *rounds corner of driveway, walking rapidly.*
JIM *crosses to* CHRIS, *motions him and pulls him down ex-
citedly.* KELLER *stands just inside kitchen door, watching
them.*]

CHRIS: What's the matter? Where is he?

JIM: Where's your mother?

CHRIS: Upstairs, dressing.

ANN [*crossing to them rapidly*]: What happened to George?

JIM: I asked him to wait in the car. Listen to me now. Can
 you take some advice? [*They wait.*] Don't bring him in here.

ANN: Why?

JIM: Kate is in bad shape, you can't explode this in front of her.

ANN: Explode what?

JIM: You know why he's here, don't try to kid it away.
 There's blood in his eye; drive him somewhere and talk to
 him alone.

[ANN *turns to go up drive, takes a couple of steps, sees*
KELLER, *and stops. He goes quietly on into house.*]

CHRIS [*shaken, and therefore angered*]: Don't be an old lady.

JIM: He's come to take her home. What does that mean? [*To*
 ANN] You know what that means. Fight it out with him
 some place else.

ANN [*comes back down towards* CHRIS]: I'll drive ... him somewhere.

CHRIS [*goes to her*]: No.

JIM: Will you stop being an idiot?

CHRIS: Nobody's afraid of him here. Cut that out!

[*He starts for driveway, but is brought up short by* GEORGE, *who enters there.* GEORGE *is* CHRIS's *age, but a paler man, now on the edge of his self-restraint. He speaks quietly, as though afraid to find himself screaming. An instant's hesitation and* CHRIS *steps up to him, hand extended, smiling.*]

CHRIS: Helluva way to do; what're you sitting out there for?

GEORGE: Doctor said your mother isn't well, I –

CHRIS: So what? She'd want to see you, wouldn't she? We've been waiting for you all afternoon. [*He puts his hand on* GEORGE's *arm, but* GEORGE *pulls away, coming across towards* ANN.]

ANN [*touching his collar*]: This is filthy, didn't you bring another shirt?

[GEORGE *breaks away from her, and moves down, examining the yard. Door opens, and he turns rapidly, thinking it is* KATE, *but it's* SUE. *She looks at him; he turns away and moves to fence. He looks over it at his former home.* SUE *comes downstage.*]

SUE [*annoyed*]: How about the beach, Jim?

JIM: Oh, it's too hot to drive.

SUE: How'd you get to the station – Zeppelin?

CHRIS: This is Mrs Bayliss, George. [*Calling, as* GEORGE *pays no attention, staring at house*] George! [GEORGE *turns.*] Mrs Bayliss.

SUE: How do you do.

GEORGE [*removing his hat*]: You're the people who bought our house, aren't you?

SUE: That's right. Come and see what we did with it before you leave.

GEORGE [*walks down and away from her*]: I liked it the way it was.

SUE [*after a brief pause*]: He's frank, isn't he?

JIM [*pulling her off*]: See you later. ... Take it easy, fella. [*They exit.*]

CHRIS [*calling after them*]: Thanks for driving him! [*Turning to* GEORGE] How about some grape juice? Mother made it especially for you.

GEORGE [*with forced appreciation*]: Good old Kate, remembered my grape juice.

CHRIS: You drank enough of it in this house. How've you been, George? – Sit down.

GEORGE [*keeps moving*]: It takes me a minute. [*Looking around*] It seems impossible.

CHRIS: What?

GEORGE: I'm back here.

CHRIS: Say, you've gotten a little nervous, haven't you?

GEORGE: Yeah, towards the end of the day. What're you, big executive now?

CHRIS: Just kind of medium. How's the law?

GEORGE: I don't know. When I was studying in the hospital it seemed sensible, but outside there doesn't seem to be much of a law. The trees got thick, didn't they? [*Points to stump.*] What's that?

CHRIS: Blew down last night. We had it there for Larry. You know.

GEORGE: Why, afraid you'll forget him?

CHRIS [*starts for* GEORGE]: Kind of a remark is that?

ANN [*breaking in, putting a restraining hand on* CHRIS]: When did you start wearing a hat?

GEORGE [*discovers hat in his hand*]: Today. From now on I decided to look like a lawyer, anyway. [*He holds it up to her.*] Don't you recognize it?

ANN: Why? Where – ?

GEORGE: Your father's – He asked me to wear it.

ANN: How is he?

GEORGE: He got smaller.

ANN: Smaller?

GEORGE: Yeah, little. [*Holds out his hand to measure.*] He's a little man. That's what happens to suckers, you know. It's good I went to him in time – another year there'd be nothing left but his smell.

CHRIS: What's the matter, George, what's the trouble?

GEORGE: The trouble? The trouble is when you make suckers out of people once, you shouldn't try to do it twice.

CHRIS: What does that mean?

GEORGE [*to* ANN]: You're not married yet, are you?

ANN: George, will you sit down and stop – ?

GEORGE: Are you married yet?

ANN: No, I'm not married yet.

GEORGE: You're not going to marry him.

ANN: Why am I not going to marry him?

GEORGE: Because his father destroyed your family.

CHRIS: Now look, George ...

GEORGE: Cut it short, Chris. Tell her to come home with me. Let's not argue, you know what I've got to say.

CHRIS: George, you don't want to be the voice of God, do you?

GEORGE: I'm –

CHRIS: That's been your trouble all your life, George, you dive into things. What kind of a statement is that to make? You're a big boy now.

GEORGE: I'm a big boy now.

CHRIS: Don't come bulling in here. If you've got something to say, be civilized about it.

GEORGE: Don't civilize me!

ANN: Shhh!

CHRIS [*ready to hit him*]: Are you going to talk like a grown man or aren't you?

ANN [*quickly, to forestall an outburst*]: Sit down, dear. Don't be angry, what's the matter? [*He allows her to seat him, looking at her.*] Now what happened? You kissed me when I left, now you –

GEORGE [*breathlessly*]: My life turned upside down since then.
I couldn't go back to work when you left. I wanted to go
to Dad and tell him you were going to be married. It
seemed impossible not to tell him. He loved you so much.
[*He pauses.*] Annie – we did a terrible thing. We can never
be forgiven. Not even to send him a card at Christmas. I
didn't see him once since I got home from the war! Annie,
you don't know what was done to that man. You don't
know what happened.

ANN [*afraid*]: Of course I know.

GEORGE: You can't know, you wouldn't be here. Dad came
to work that day. The night foreman came to him and
showed him the cylinder heads ... they were coming out
of the process with defects. There was something wrong
with the process. So Dad went directly to the phone and
called here and told Joe to come down right away. But the
morning passed. No sign of Joe. So Dad called again. By
this time he had over a hundred defectives. The Army was
screaming for stuff and Dad didn't have anything to ship.
So Joe told him ... on the phone he told him to weld,
cover up the cracks in any way he could, and ship them out.

CHRIS: Are you through now?

GEORGE [*surging up at him*]: I'm not through now! [*Back to*
ANN] Dad was afraid. He wanted Joe there if he was going
to do it. But Joe can't come down ... He's sick. Sick! He
suddenly gets the flu! Suddenly! But he promised to take
responsibility. Do you understand what I'm saying? On the
telephone you can't have responsibility! In a court you can
always deny a phone call and that's exactly what he did.
They knew he was a liar the first time, but in the appeal they
believed that rotten lie and now Joe is a big shot and your
father is the patsy. [*He gets up.*] Now what're you going to
do? Eat his food, sleep in his bed? Answer me; what're you
going to do?

CHRIS: What're you going to do, George?

GEORGE: He's too smart for me, I can't prove a phone call.

CHRIS: Then how dare you come in here with that rot?

ANN: George, the court –

GEORGE: The court didn't know your father! But you know him. You know in your heart Joe did it.

CHRIS [whirling him around]: Lower your voice or I'll throw you out of here!

GEORGE: She knows. She knows.

CHRIS [to ANN]: Get him out of here, Ann. Get him out of here.

ANN: George, I know everything you've said. Dad told that whole thing in court, and they –

GEORGE [– almost a scream]: The court did not know him, Annie!

ANN: Shhh! – But he'll say anything, George. You know how quick he can lie.

GEORGE [turning to CHRIS, with deliberation]: I'll ask you something, and look me in the eye when you answer me.

CHRIS: I'll look you in the eye.

GEORGE: You know your father –

CHRIS: I know him well.

GEORGE: And he's the kind of boss to let a hundred and twenty-one cylinder heads be repaired and shipped out of his shop without even knowing about it?

CHRIS: He's that kind of boss.

GEORGE: And that's the same Joe Keller who never left his shop without first going around to see that all the lights were out.

CHRIS [with growing anger]: The same Joe Keller.

GEORGE: The same man who knows how many minutes a day his workers spend in the toilet.

CHRIS: The same man.

GEORGE: And my father, that frightened mouse who'd never

buy a shirt without somebody along – that man would dare
do such a thing on his own?

CHRIS: On his own. And because he's a frightened mouse this
is another thing he'd do – throw the blame on somebody
else because he's not man enough to take it himself. He
tried it in court but it didn't work, but with a fool like you
it works!

GEORGE: Oh, Chris, you're a liar to yourself!

ANN [deeply shaken]: Don't talk like that!

CHRIS [sits facing GEORGE]: Tell me, George. What happened?
The court record was good enough for you all these years,
why isn't it good now? Why did you believe it all these
years?

GEORGE [after a slight pause]: Because you believed it ....
That's the truth, Chris. I believed everything, because I
thought you did. But today I heard it from his mouth.
From his mouth it's altogether different than the record.
Anyone who knows him, and knows your father, will believe it from his mouth. Your Dad took everything we
have. I can't beat that. But she's one item he's not going to
grab. [He turns to ANN.] Get your things. Everything they
have is covered with blood. You're not the kind of a girl
who can live with that. Get your things.

CHRIS: Ann ... you're not going to believe that, are you?

ANN [goes to him]: You know it's not true, don't you?

GEORGE: How can he tell you? It's his father. [To CHRIS]
None of these things ever even cross your mind?

CHRIS: Yes, they crossed my mind. Anything can cross your
mind!

GEORGE: He knows, Annie! He knows!

CHRIS: The voice of God!

GEORGE: Then why isn't your name on the business? Explain
that to her!

CHRIS: What the hell has that got to do with – ?

GEORGE: Annie, why isn't his name on it?

CHRIS: Even when I don't own it!

GEORGE: Who're you kidding? Who gets it when he dies?
[*To* ANN] Open your eyes, you know the both of them, isn't
that the first thing they'd do, the way they love each other?
– J. O. Keller and Son? [*Pause.* ANN *looks from him to* CHRIS.]
I'll settle it. Do you want to settle it, or are you afraid to?

CHRIS: What do you mean?

GEORGE: Let me go up and talk to your father. In ten minutes
you'll have the answer. Or are you afraid of the answer?

CHRIS: I'm not afraid of the answer. I know the answer. But
my mother isn't well and I don't want a fight here now.

GEORGE: Let me go to him.

CHRIS: You're not going to start a fight here now.

GEORGE [*to* ANN]: What more do you want! [*There is a sound
of footsteps in the house.*]

ANN [*turns her head suddenly towards house*]: Someone's coming.

CHRIS [*to* GEORGE, *quietly*]: You won't say anything now.

ANN: You'll go soon. I'll call a cab.

GEORGE: You're coming with me.

ANN: And don't mention marriage, because we haven't told
her yet.

GEORGE: You're coming with me.

ANN: You understand? Don't – George, you're not going to
start anything now! [*She hears footsteps.*] Shsh!
[MOTHER *enters on porch. She is dressed almost formally; her
hair is fixed. They are all turned towards her. On seeing*
GEORGE *she raises both hands, comes down towards him.*]

MOTHER: Georgie, Georgie.

GEORGE [– *he has always liked her*]: Hello, Kate.

MOTHER [*cups his face in her hands*]: They made an old man
out of you. [*Touches his hair.*] Look, you're grey.

GEORGE [– *her pity, open and unabashed, reaches into him, and he
smiles sadly*]: I know, I –

MOTHER: I told you when you went away, don't try for medals.

GEORGE [*laughs, tiredly*]: I didn't try, Kate. They made it very easy for me.

MOTHER [*actually angry*]: Go on. You're all alike. [*To* ANN] Look at him, why did you say he's fine? He looks like a ghost.

GEORGE [*relishing her solicitude*]: I feel all right.

MOTHER: I'm sick to look at you. What's the matter with your mother, why don't she feed you?

ANN: He just hasn't any appetite.

MOTHER: If he ate in my house he'd have an appetite. [*To* ANN] I pity your husband! [*To* GEORGE] Sit down. I'll make you a sandwich.

GEORGE [– *sits with an embarrassed laugh*]: I'm really not hungry.

MOTHER: Honest to God, it breaks my heart to see what happened to all the children. How we worked and planned for you, and you end up no better than us.

GEORGE [*with deep feeling for her*]: You ... you haven't changed at all, you know that, Kate?

MOTHER: None of us changed, Georgie. We all love you. Joe was just talking about the day you were born and the water got shut off. People were carrying basins from a block away – a stranger would have thought the whole neighbourhood was on fire! [*They laugh. She sees the juice. To* ANN] Why didn't you give him some juice!

ANN [*defensively*]: I offered it to him.

MOTHER [*scoffingly*]: You offered it to him! [*Thrusting glass into* GEORGE's *hand*] Give it to him! [*To* GEORGE, *who is laughing*] And now you're going to sit here and drink some juice ... and look like something!

GEORGE [*sitting*]: Kate, I feel hungry already.

CHRIS [*proudly*]: She could turn Mahatma Gandhi into a heavyweight!

MOTHER [*to* CHRIS, *with great energy*]: Listen, to hell with the restaurant! I got a ham in the icebox, and frozen strawberries, and avocados, and –

ANN: Swell, I'll help you!

GEORGE: The train leaves at eight-thirty, Ann.

MOTHER [*to* ANN]: You're leaving?

CHRIS: No, Mother, she's not –

ANN [*breaking through it, going to* GEORGE]: You hardly got here; give yourself a chance to get acquainted again.

CHRIS: Sure, you don't even know us any more.

MOTHER: Well, Chris, if they can't stay, don't –

CHRIS: No, it's just a question of George, Mother, he planned on –

GEORGE [*gets up politely, nicely, for* KATE'*s sake*]: Now wait a minute, Chris …

CHRIS [*smiling, and full of command, cutting him off*]: If you want to go, I'll drive you to the station now, but if you're staying, no arguments while you're here.

MOTHER [*at last confessing the tension*]: Why should he argue? [*She goes to him. With desperation and compassion, stroking his hair*] Georgie and us have no argument. How could we have an argument, Georgie? We all got hit by the same lightning, how can you – ? Did you see what happened to Larry's tree, Georgie? [*She has taken his arm, and unwillingly he moves across stage with her.*] Imagine? While I was dreaming of him in the middle of the night, the wind came along and –

[LYDIA *enters on porch. As soon as she sees him*]

LYDIA: Hey, Georgie! Georgie! Georgie! Georgie! Georgie! [*She comes down to him eagerly. She has a flowered hat in her hand, which* KATE *takes from her as she goes to* GEORGE.]

GEORGE [*as they shake hands eagerly, warmly*]: Hello, Laughy. What'd you do, grow?

LYDIA: I'm a big girl now.

MOTHER: Look what she can do to a hat!

ANN [to LYDIA, *admiring the hat*]: Did you make that?

MOTHER: In ten minutes! [*She puts it on.*]

LYDIA [*fixing it on her head*]: I only rearranged it.

GEORGE: You still make your own clothes?

CHRIS [*of* MOTHER]: Ain't she classy! All she needs now is a Russian wolfhound.

MOTHER [*moving her head*]: It feels like somebody is sitting on my head.

ANN: No, it's beautiful, Kate.

MOTHER [*kisses* LYDIA. *To* GEORGE]: She's a genius! You should've married her. [*They laugh.*] This one can feed you!

LYDIA [*strangely embarrassed*]: Oh, stop that, Kate.

GEORGE [*to* LYDIA]: Didn't I hear you had a baby?

MOTHER: You don't hear so good. She's got three babies.

GEORGE [*a little hurt by it – to* LYDIA]: No kidding, three?

LYDIA: Yeah, it was one, two, three – You've been away a long time, Georgie.

GEORGE: I'm beginning to realize.

MOTHER [*to* CHRIS *and* GEORGE]: The trouble with you kids is you *think* too much.

LYDIA: Well, we think, too.

MOTHER: Yes, but not all the time.

GEORGE [*with almost obvious envy*]: They never took Frank, heh?

LYDIA [*a little apologetically*]: No, he was always one year ahead of the draft.

MOTHER: It's amazing. When they were calling boys twenty-seven Frank was just twenty-eight, when they made it twenty-eight he was just twenty-nine. That's why he took up astrology. It's all in when you were born, it just goes to show.

CHRIS: What does it go to show?

MOTHER [*to* CHRIS]: Don't be so intelligent. Some supersti-
tions are very nice! [*To* LYDIA] Did he finish Larry's
horoscope?

LYDIA: I'll ask him now, I'm going in. [*To* GEORGE, *a little
sadly, almost embarrassed*] Would you like to see my babies?
Come on.

GEORGE: I don't think so, Lydia.

LYDIA [*understanding*]: All right. Good luck to you, George.

GEORGE: Thanks. And to you ... and Frank. [*She smiles at
him, turns and goes off to her house.* GEORGE *stands staring after
her.*]

LYDIA [*as she runs off*]: Oh, Frank!

MOTHER [*reading his thoughts*]: She got pretty, heh?

GEORGE [*sadly*]: Very pretty.

MOTHER [*as a reprimand*]: She's beautiful, you damned fool!

GEORGE [*looks around longingly; and softly, with a catch in his
throat*]: She makes it seem so nice around here.

MOTHER [*shaking her finger at him*]: Look what happened to
you because you wouldn't listen to me! I told you to marry
that girl and stay out of the war!

GEORGE [*laughs at himself*]: She used to laugh too much.

MOTHER: And you didn't laugh enough. While you were
getting mad about Fascism Frank was getting into her bed.

GEORGE [*to* CHRIS]: He won the war, Frank.

CHRIS: All the battles.

MOTHER [*in pursuit of this mood*]: The day they started the
draft, Georgie, I told you you loved that girl.

CHRIS [*laughs*]: And truer love hath no man!

MOTHER: I'm smarter than any of you.

GEORGIE [*laughing*]: She's wonderful!

MOTHER: And now you're going to listen to me, George.
You had big principles, Eagle Scouts the three of you; so
now I got a tree, and this one [*indicating* CHRIS] when the
weather gets bad he can't stand on his feet; and that big

dope [*pointing to* LYDIA's *house*] next door who never reads anything but Andy Gump has three children and his house paid off. Stop being a philosopher, and look after yourself. Like Joe was just saying – you move back here, he'll help you get set, and I'll find you a girl and put a smile on your face.

GEORGE: Joe? Joe wants me here?

ANN [*eagerly*]: He asked me to tell you, and I think it's a good idea.

MOTHER: Certainly. Why must you make believe you hate us? Is that another principle? – that you have to hate us? You don't hate us, George, I know you, you can't fool me, I diapered you. [*Suddenly to* ANN] You remember Mr Marcy's daughter?

ANN [*laughing, to* GEORGE]: She's got you hooked already! [GEORGE *laughs, is excited.*]

MOTHER: You look her over, George; you'll see she's the most beautiful –

CHRIS: She's got warts, George.

MOTHER [*to* CHRIS]: She hasn't got warts! [*To* GEORGE] So the girl has a little beauty mark on her chin –

CHRIS: And two on her nose.

MOTHER: You remember. Her father's the retired police inspector.

CHRIS: Sergeant, George.

MOTHER: He's a very kind man!

CHRIS: He looks like a gorilla.

MOTHER [*to* GEORGE]: He never shot anybody.
  [*They all burst out laughing, as* KELLER *appears in doorway.* GEORGE *rises abruptly and stares at* KELLER, *who comes rapidly down to him.*]

KELLER [*– the laughter stops. With strained joviality*]: Well! Look who's here! [*Extending his hand*] Georgie, good to see ya.

GEORGE [*shaking hands – sombrely*]: How're you, Joe?

KELLER: So-so. Gettin' old. You comin' out to dinner with us?

GEORGE: No, got to be back in New York.

ANN: I'll call a cab for you. [*She goes up into the house.*]

KELLER: Too bad you can't stay, George. Sit down. [*To* MOTHER] He looks fine.

MOTHER: He looks terrible.

KELLER: That's what I said, you look terrible, George. [*They laugh.*] I wear the pants and she beats me with the belt.

GEORGE: I saw your factory on the way from the station. It looks like General Motors.

KELLER: I wish it was General Motors, but it ain't. Sit down, George. Sit down. [*Takes cigar out of his pocket.*] So you finally went to see your father, I hear?

GEORGE: Yes, this morning. What kind of stuff do you make now?

KELLER: Oh, little of everything. Pressure-cookers, an assembly for washing-machines. Got a nice, flexible plant now. So how'd you find Dad? Feel all right?

GEORGE [*searching* KELLER, *speaking indecisively*]: No, he's not well, Joe.

KELLER [*lighting his cigar*]: Not his heart again, is it?

GEORGE: It's everything, Joe. It's his soul.

KELLER [*blowing out smoke*]: Uh huh –

CHRIS: How about seeing what they did with your house?

KELLER: Leave him be.

GEORGE [*to* CHRIS, *indicating* KELLER]: I'd like to talk to him.

KELLER: Sure, he just got here. That's the way they do, George. A little man makes a mistake and they hang him by the thumbs; the big ones become ambassadors. I wish you'd-a told me you were going to see Dad.

GEORGE [*studying him*]: I didn't know you were interested.

KELLER: In a way, I am. I would like him to know, George, that as far as I'm concerned, any time he wants, he's got a place with me. I would like him to know that.

GEORGE: He hates your guts, Joe. Don't you know that?

KELLER: I imagined it. But that can change, too.

MOTHER: Steve was never like that.

GEORGE: He's like that now. He'd like to take every man who made money in the war and put him up against a wall.

CHRIS: He'll need a lot of bullets.

GEORGE: And he'd better not get any.

KELLER: That's a sad thing to hear.

GEORGE [*with bitterness dominant*]: Why? What'd you expect him to think of you?

KELLER [– *the force of his nature rising, but under control*]: I'm sad to see he hasn't changed. As long as I know him, twenty-five years, the man never learned how to take the blame. You know that, George.

GEORGE [– *he does*]: Well, I –

KELLER: But you do know it. Because the way you come in here you don't look like you remember it. I mean like in 1937 when we had the shop on Flood Street. And he damn near blew us all up with that heater he left burning for two days without water. He wouldn't admit that was his fault, either. I had to fire a mechanic to save his face. You remember that.

GEORGE: Yes, but –

KELLER: I'm just mentioning it, George. Because this is just another one of a lot of things. Like when he gave Frank that money to invest in oil stock.

GEORGE [*distressed*]: I know that, I –

KELLER [*driving in, but restrained*]: But it's good to remember those things, kid. The way he cursed Frank because the stock went down. Was that Frank's fault? To listen to him Frank was a swindler. And all the man did was give him a bad tip.

GEORGE [*gets up, moves away*]: I know those things. ...

KELLER: Then remember them, remember them. [ANN *comes*

out of house.] There are certain men in the world who rather see everybody hung before they'll take blame. You understand me, George?

[*They stand facing each other,* GEORGE *trying to judge him.*]

ANN [*coming downstage*]: The cab's on its way. Would you like to wash?

MOTHER [*with the thrust of hope*]: Why must he go? Make the midnight, George.

KELLER: Sure, you'll have dinner with us!

ANN: How about it? Why not? We're eating at the lake, we could have a swell time.

[*A long pause, as* GEORGE *looks at* ANN, CHRIS, KELLER, *then back at her.*]

GEORGE: All right.

MOTHER: Now you're talking.

CHRIS: I've got a shirt that'll go right with that suit.

MOTHER: Size fifteen and a half, right, George?

GEORGE: Is Lydia – ? I mean – Frank and Lydia coming?

MOTHER: I'll get you a date that'll make her look like a – [*She starts upstage.*]

GEORGE [*laughing*]: No, I don't want a date.

CHRIS: I know somebody just for you! Charlotte Tanner! [*He starts for the house.*]

KELLER: Call Charlotte, that's right.

MOTHER: Sure, call her up. [CHRIS *goes into house.*]

ANN: You go up and pick out a shirt and tie.

GEORGE [*stops, looks around at them and the place*]: I never felt at home anywhere but here. I feel so – [*He nearly laughs, and turns away from them.*] Kate, you look so young, you know? You didn't change at all. It … rings an old bell. [*Turns to* KELLER.] You too, Joe, you're amazingly the same. The whole atmosphere is.

KELLER: Say, I ain't got time to get sick.

MOTHER: He hasn't been laid up in fifteen years.

KELLER: Except my flu during the war.

MOTHER: Huhh?

KELLER: My flu, when I was sick during . . . the war.

MOTHER: Well, sure ... [*To* GEORGE] I mean except for that flu. [GEORGE *stands perfectly still.*] Well, it slipped my mind, don't look at me that way. He wanted to go to the shop but he couldn't lift himself off the bed. I thought he had pneumonia.

GEORGE: Why did you say he's never – ?

KELLER: I know how you feel, kid, I'll never forgive myself. If I could've gone in that day I'd never allow Dad to touch those heads.

GEORGE: She said you've never been sick.

MOTHER: I said he was sick, George.

GEORGE [*going to* ANN]: Ann, didn't you hear her say – ?

MOTHER: Do you remember every time you were sick?

GEORGE: I'd remember pneumonia. Especially if I got it just the day my partner was going to patch up cylinder heads. ... What happened that day, Joe?

[FRANK *enters briskly from driveway, holding Larry's horoscope in his hand. He comes to* KATE.]

FRANK: Kate! Kate!

MOTHER: Frank, did you see George?

FRANK [*extending his hand*]: Lydia told me, I'm glad to . . . you'll have to pardon me. [*Pulling* MOTHER *over*] I've got something amazing for you, Kate, I finished Larry's horoscope.

MOTHER: You'd be interested in this, George. It's wonderful the way he can understand the –

CHRIS [*entering from house*]: George, the girl's on the phone –

MOTHER [*desperately*]: He finished Larry's horoscope!

CHRIS: Frank, can't you pick a better time than this?

FRANK: The greatest men who ever lived believed in the stars!

CHRIS: Stop filling her head with that junk!

FRANK: Is it junk to feel that there's a greater power than our-selves? I've studied the stars of his life! I won't argue with you, I'm telling you. Somewhere in this world your brother is alive!

MOTHER [*instantly to* CHRIS]: Why isn't it possible?

CHRIS: Because it's insane.

FRANK: Just a minute now. I'll tell you something and you can do as you please. Just let me say it. He was supposed to have died on November twenty-fifth. But November twenty-fifth was his favourable day.

CHRIS: Mother!

MOTHER: Listen to him!

FRANK: It was a day when everything good was shining on him, the kind of day he should've married on. You can laugh at a lot of it, I can understand you laughing. But the odds are a million to one that a man won't die on his favourable day. That's known, that's known, Chris!

MOTHER: Why isn't it possible, why isn't it possible, Chris!

GEORGE [*to* ANN]: Don't you understand what she's saying? She just told you to go. What are you waiting for now?

CHRIS: Nobody can tell her to go. [*A car horn is heard.*]

MOTHER [*to* FRANK]: Thank you, darling, for your trouble. Will you tell him to wait, Frank?

FRANK [*as he goes*]: Sure thing.

MOTHER [*calling out*]: They'll be right out, driver!

CHRIS: She's not leaving, Mother.

GEORGE: You heard her say it, he's never been sick!

MOTHER: He misunderstood me, Chris! [CHRIS *looks at her, struck.*]

GEORGE [*to* ANN]: He simply told your father to kill pilots, and covered himself in bed!

CHRIS: You'd better answer him, Annie. Answer him.

MOTHER: I packed your bag, darling.

CHRIS: What?

MOTHER: I packed your bag. All you've got to do is close it.

ANN: I'm not closing anything. He asked me here and I'm staying till he tells me to go. [*To* GEORGE] Till Chris tells me!

CHRIS: That's all! Now get out of here, George!

MOTHER [*to* CHRIS]: But if that's how he feels –

CHRIS: That's all, nothing more till Christ comes, about the case or Larry as long as I'm here! [*To* GEORGE] Now get out of here, George!

GEORGE [*to* ANN]: You tell me. I want to hear you tell me.

ANN: Go, George!

[*They disappear up the driveway,* ANN *saying,* '*Don't take it that way, Georgie! Please don't take it that way.*']

CHRIS [*turning to his* MOTHER]: What do you mean, you packed her bag? How dare you pack her bag?

MOTHER: Chris –

CHRIS: How dare you pack her bag?

MOTHER: She doesn't belong here.

CHRIS: Then I don't belong here.

MOTHER: She's Larry's girl.

CHRIS: And I'm his brother and he's dead, and I'm marrying his girl.

MOTHER: Never, never in this world!

KELLER: You lost your mind?

MOTHER: You have nothing to say!

KELLER [*cruelly*]: I got plenty to say. Three and a half years you been talking like a maniac –

[MOTHER *smashes him across the face.*]

MOTHER: Nothing. You have nothing to say. Now I say. He's coming back, and everybody has got to wait.

CHRIS: Mother, Mother –

MOTHER: Wait, wait –

CHRIS: How long? How long?

MOTHER [*rolling out of her*]: Till he comes; for ever and ever till he comes!

CHRIS [*as an ultimatum*]: Mother, I'm going ahead with it.

MOTHER: Chris, I've never said no to you in my life, now I say no!

CHRIS: You'll never let him go till I do it.

MOTHER: I'll never let him go and you'll never let him go!

CHRIS: I've let him go. I've let him go a long –

MOTHER [*with no less force, but turning from him*]: Then let your father go. [*Pause.* CHRIS *stands transfixed.*]

KELLER: She's out of her mind.

MOTHER: Altogether! [*To* CHRIS, *but not facing them*] Your brother's alive, darling, because if he's dead, your father killed him. Do you understand me now? As long as you live, that boy is alive. God does not let a son be killed by his father. Now you see, don't you? Now you see. [*Beyond control, she hurries up and into house.*]

KELLER [– CHRIS *has not moved. He speaks insinuatingly, questioningly*]: She's out of her mind.

CHRIS [*in a broken whisper*]: Then ... you did it?

KELLER [*with the beginning of plea in his voice*]: He never flew a P-40 –

CHRIS [*struck; deadly*]: But the others.

KELLER [*insistently*]: She's out of her mind. [*He takes a step towards* CHRIS, *pleadingly.*]

CHRIS [*unyielding*]: Dad ... you did it?

KELLER: He never flew a P-40, what's the matter with you?

CHRIS [*still asking, and saying*]: Then you did it. To the others. [*Both hold their voices down.*]

KELLER [*afraid of him, his deadly insistence*]: What's the matter with you? What the hell is the matter with you?

CHRIS [*quietly, incredibly*]: How could you do that? How?

KELLER: What's the matter with you!

CHRIS: Dad ... Dad, you killed twenty-one men!

KELLER: What, killed?

CHRIS: You killed them, you murdered them.

KELLER [*as though throwing his whole nature open before* CHRIS]: How could I kill anybody?

CHRIS: Dad! Dad!

KELLER [*trying to hush him*]: I didn't kill anybody!

CHRIS: Then explain it to me. What did you do? Explain it to me or I'll tear you to pieces!

KELLER [*horrified at his overwhelming fury*]: Don't, Chris, don't –

CHRIS: I want to know what you did, now what did you do? You had a hundred and twenty cracked engine-heads, now what did you do?

KELLER: If you're going to hang me then I –

CHRIS: I'm listening. God Almighty, I'm listening!

KELLER [– *their movements now are those of subtle pursuit and escape.* KELLER *keeps a step out of* CHRIS's *range as he talks*.]: You're a boy, what could I do! I'm in business, a man is in business; a hundred and twenty cracked, you're out of business; you got a process, the process don't work you're out of business; you don't know how to operate, your stuff is no good; they close you up, they tear up your contracts, what the hell's it to them? You lay forty years into a business and they knock you out in five minutes, what could I do, let them take forty years, let them take my life away? [*His voice cracking*] I never thought they'd install them. I swear to God. I thought they'd stop 'em before anybody took off.

CHRIS: Then why'd you ship them out?

KELLER: By the time they could spot them I thought I'd have the process going again, and I could show them they needed me and they'd let it go by. But weeks passed and I got no kick-back, so I was going to tell them.

CHRIS: Then why didn't you tell them?

KELLER: It was too late. The paper, it was all over the front page, twenty-one went down, it was too late. They came with handcuffs into the shop, what could I do? [*He sits on bench.*] Chris ... Chris, I did it for you, it was a chance and I took it for you. I'm sixty-one years old, when would I have another chance to make something for you? Sixty-one years old you don't get another chance, do ya?

CHRIS: You even knew they wouldn't hold up in the air.

KELLER: I didn't say that.

CHRIS: But you were going to warn them not to use them –

KELLER: But that don't mean –

CHRIS: It means you knew they'd crash.

KELLER: It don't mean that.

CHRIS: Then you *thought* they'd crash.

KELLER: I was afraid maybe –

CHRIS: You were afraid maybe! God in heaven, what kind of a man are you? Kids were hanging in the air by those heads. You knew that!

KELLER: For you, a business for you!

CHRIS [*with burning fury*]: For me! Where do you live, where have you come from? For me! – I was dying every day and you were killing my boys and you did it for me? What the hell do you think I was thinking of, the goddam business? Is that as far as your mind can see, the business? What is that, the world – the business? What the hell do you mean, you did it for me? Don't you have a country? Don't you live in the world? What the hell are you? You're not even an animal, no animal kills his own, what are you? What must I do to you? I ought to tear the tongue out of your mouth, what must I do? [*With his fist he pounds down upon his father's shoulder. He stumbles away, covering his face as he weeps.*] What must I do, Jesus God, what must I do?

KELLER: Chris ... My Chris ...

CURTAIN

ACT THREE

[*Two o'clock the following morning.* MOTHER *is discovered on the rise, rocking ceaselessly in a chair, staring at her thoughts. It is an intense, slight sort of rocking. A light shows from upstairs bedroom, lower floor windows being dark. The moon is strong and casts its bluish light.*

Presently JIM *dressed in jacket and hat, appears, and seeing her, goes up beside her.*]

JIM: Any news?

MOTHER: No news.

JIM [*gently*]: You can't sit up all night, dear, why don't you go to bed?

MOTHER: I'm waiting for Chris. Don't worry about me, Jim, I'm perfectly all right.

JIM: But it's almost two o'clock.

MOTHER: I can't sleep. [*Slight pause.*] You had an emergency?

JIM [*tiredly*]: Somebody had a headache and thought he was dying. [*Slight pause.*] Half of my patients are quite mad. Nobody realizes how many people are walking around loose, and they're cracked as coconuts. Money. Money-money-money-money. You say it long enough it doesn't mean anything. [*She smiles, makes a silent laugh.*] Oh, how I'd love to be around when that happens!

MOTHER [*shaking her head*]: You're so childish, Jim! Sometimes you are.

JIM [*looks at her a moment*]: Kate. [*Pause.*] What happened?

MOTHER: I told you. He had an argument with Joe. Then he got in the car and drove away.

JIM: What kind of an argument?

MOTHER: An argument, Joe ... He was crying like a child, before.

JIM: They argued about Ann?

MOTHER [*after slight hesitation*]: No, not Ann. Imagine? [*Indicates lighted window above.*] She hasn't come out of that room since he left. All night in that room.

JIM [*looks at window, then at her*]: What'd Joe do, tell him?

MOTHER [*stops rocking*]: Tell him what?

JIM: Don't be afraid, Kate, I know. I've always known.

MOTHER: How?

JIM: It occurred to me a long time ago.

MOTHER: I always had the feeling that in the back of his head, Chris ... almost knew. I didn't think it would be such a shock.

JIM [*gets up*]: Chris would never know how to live with a thing like that. It takes a certain talent – for lying. You have it, and I do. But not him.

MOTHER: What do you mean ... ? He's not coming back?

JIM: Oh, no, he'll come back. We all come back, Kate. These private little revolutions always die. The compromise is always made. In a peculiar way, Frank is right – every man does have a star. The star of one's honesty. And you spend your life groping for it, but once it's out it never lights again. I don't think he went very far. He probably just wanted to be alone to watch his star go out.

MOTHER: Just as long as he comes back.

JIM: I wish he wouldn't, Kate. One year I simply took off, went to New Orleans; for two months I lived on bananas and milk, and studied a certain disease. It was beautiful. And then she came, and she cried. And I went back home with her. And now I live in the usual darkness; I can't find myself; it's even hard sometimes to remember the kind of man I wanted to be. I'm a good husband; Chris is a good son – he'll come back.

[KELLER *comes out on porch in dressing-gown and slippers. He goes upstage – to alley.* JIM *goes to him.*]

JIM: I have a feeling he's in the park. I'll look around for him. Put her to bed, Joe; this is no good for what she's got. [JIM *exits up driveway.*]

KELLER [*coming down*]: What does he want here?

MOTHER: His friend is not home.

KELLER [*comes down to her. His voice is husky.*]: I don't like him mixing in so much.

MOTHER: It's too late, Joe. He knows.

KELLER [*apprehensively*]: How does he know?

MOTHER: He guessed a long time ago.

KELLER: I don't like that.

MOTHER [*laughs dangerously, quietly into the line*]: What you don't like.

KELLER: Yeah, what I don't like.

MOTHER: You can't bull yourself through this one, Joe, you better be smart now. This thing – this thing is not over yet.

KELLER [*indicating lighted window above*]: And what is she doing up there? She don't come out of the room.

MOTHER: I don't know, what is she doing? Sit down, stop being mad. You want to live? You better figure out your life.

KELLER: She don't know, does she?

MOTHER: She saw Chris storming out of here. It's one and one – she knows how to add.

KELLER: Maybe I ought to talk to her?

MOTHER: Don't ask me, Joe.

KELLER [– *almost an outburst*]: Then who do I ask? But I don't think she'll do anything about it.

MOTHER: You're asking me again.

KELLER: I'm askin' you. What am I, a stranger? I thought I had a family here. What happened to my family?

MOTHER: You've got a family. I'm simply telling you that I have no strength to think any more.

KELLER: You have no strength. The minute there's trouble you have no strength.

MOTHER: Joe, you're doing the same thing again; all your life whenever there's trouble you yell at me and you think that settles it.

KELLER: Then what do I do? Tell me, talk to me, what do I do?

MOTHER: Joe ... I've been thinking this way. If he comes back –

KELLER: What do you mean 'if'? He's comin' back!

MOTHER: I think if you sit him down and you – explain yourself. I mean you ought to make it clear to him that you know you did a terrible thing. [*Not looking into his eyes*] I mean if he saw that you realize what you did. You see?

KELLER: What ice does that cut?

MOTHER [*a little fearfully*]: I mean if you told him that you want to pay for what you did.

KELLER [*sensing ... quietly*]: How can I pay?

MOTHER: Tell him – you're willing to go to prison. [*Pause.*]

KELLER [*struck, amazed*]: I'm willing to – ?

MOTHER [*quickly*]: You wouldn't go, he wouldn't ask you to go. But if you told him you wanted to, if he could feel that you wanted to pay, maybe he would forgive you.

KELLER: He would forgive me! For what?

MOTHER: Joe, you know what I mean.

KELLER: I don't know what you mean! You wanted money, so I made money. What must I be forgiven? You wanted money, didn't you?

MOTHER: I didn't want it that way.

KELLER: I didn't want it that way, either! What difference is it what you want? I spoiled the both of you. I should've put him out when he was ten like I was put out, and made him earn his keep. Then he'd know how a buck is made in this world. Forgiven! I could live on a quarter a day myself, but I got a family so I –

MOTHER: Joe, Joe ... It don't excuse it that you did it for the family.

KELLER: It's got to excuse it!

MOTHER: There's something bigger than the family to him.

KELLER: Nothin' is bigger!

MOTHER: There is to him.

KELLER: There's nothin' he could do that I wouldn't forgive. Because he's my son. Because I'm his father and he's my son.

MOTHER: Joe, I tell you –

KELLER: Nothin's bigger than that. And you're goin' to tell him, you understand? I'm his father and he's my son, and if there's something bigger than that I'll put a bullet in my head!

MOTHER: You stop that!

KELLER: You heard me. Now you know what to tell him. [Pause. He moves from her – halts.] But he wouldn't put me away though. ... He wouldn't do that ... would he?

MOTHER: He loved you, Joe, you broke his heart.

KELLER: But to put me away ...

MOTHER: I don't know. I'm beginning to think we don't really know him. They say in the war he was such a killer. Here he was always afraid of mice. I don't know him. I don't know what he'll do.

KELLER: Goddam, if Larry was alive he wouldn't act like this. He understood the way the world is made. He listened to me. To him the world had a forty-foot front, it ended at the building line. This one, everything bothers him. You make a deal, overcharge two cents, and his hair falls out. He don't understand money. Too easy, it came too easy. Yes, sir. Larry. That was a boy we lost. Larry. Larry. [*He slumps on chair in front of her.*] What am I gonna do, Kate?

MOTHER: Joe, Joe, please ... You'll be all right, nothing is going to happen.

KELLER [*desperately, lost*]: For you, Kate, for both of you, that's all I ever lived for. ...

MOTHER: I know, darling, I know. [ANN *enters from house. They say nothing, waiting for her to speak.*]

ANN: Why do you stay up? I'll tell you when he comes.

KELLER [*rises, goes to her*]: You didn't eat supper, did you? [*To* MOTHER] Why don't you make her something?

MOTHER: Sure, I'll –

ANN: Never mind, Kate, I'm all right. [*They are unable to speak to each other.*] There's something I want to tell you. [*She starts, then halts.*] I'm not going to do anything about it.

MOTHER: She's a good girl! [*To* KELLER] You see? She's a –

ANN: I'll do nothing about Joe, but you're going to do something for me. [*Directly to* MOTHER] You made Chris feel guilty with me. Whether you wanted to or not, you've crippled him in front of me. I'd like you to tell him that Larry is dead and that you know it. You understand me? I'm not going out of here alone. There's no life for me that way. I want you to set him free. And then I promise you, everything will end, and we'll go away, and that's all.

KELLER: You'll do that. You'll tell him.

ANN: I know what I'm asking, Kate. You had two sons. But you've only got one now.

KELLER: You'll tell him.

ANN: And you've got to say it to him so he knows you mean it.

MOTHER: My dear, if the boy was dead, it wouldn't depend on my words to make Chris know it. ... The night he gets into your bed, his heart will dry up. Because he knows and you know. To his dying day he'll wait for his brother! No, my dear, no such thing. You're going in the morning, and you're going alone. That's your life, that's your lonely life. [*She goes to porch, and starts in.*]

ANN: Larry is dead, Kate.

MOTHER [*– she stops*]: Don't speak to me.

ANN: I said he's dead. I know! He crashed off the coast of China November twenty-fifth! His engine didn't fail him. But he died. I know …

MOTHER: How did he die? You're lying to me. If you know, how did he die?

ANN: I loved him. You know I loved him. Would I have looked at anyone else if I wasn't sure? That's enough for you.

MOTHER [*moving on her*]: What's enough for me? What're you talking about? [*She grasps ANN's wrists.*]

ANN: You're hurting my wrists.

MOTHER: What are you talking about! [*Pause. She stares at ANN a moment, then turns and goes to KELLER.*]

ANN: Joe, go in the house.

KELLER: Why should I –

ANN: Please go.

KELLER: Lemme know when he comes. [*KELLER goes into house.*]

MOTHER [*as she sees ANN taking a letter from her pocket*]: What's that?

ANN: Sit down. [*MOTHER moves left to chair, but does not sit.*] First you've got to understand. When I came, I didn't have any idea that Joe – I had nothing against him or you. I came to get married. I hoped … So I didn't bring this to hurt you. I thought I'd show it to you only if there was no other way to settle Larry in your mind.

MOTHER: Larry? [*Snatches letter from ANN's hand.*]

ANN: He wrote it to me just before he – [*MOTHER opens and begins to read letter.*] I'm not trying to hurt you, Kate. You're making me do this, now remember you're – Remember.

I've been so lonely, Kate ... I can't leave here alone again. [*A long, low moan comes from* MOTHER's *throat as she reads.*] You made me show it to you. You wouldn't believe me. I told you a hundred times, why wouldn't you believe me!

MOTHER: Oh, my God ...

ANN [*with pity and fear*]: Kate, please, please . . .

MOTHER: My God, my God ...

ANN: Kate, dear, I'm so sorry ... I'm so sorry.

[CHRIS *enters from driveway. He seems exhausted.*]

CHRIS: What's the matter – ?

ANN: Where were you? ... You're all perspired. [MOTHER *doesn't move.*] Where were you?

CHRIS: Just drove around a little. I thought you'd be gone.

ANN: Where do I go? I have nowhere to go.

CHRIS [*to* MOTHER]: Where's Dad?

ANN: Inside lying down.

CHRIS: Sit down, both of you. I'll say what there is to say.

MOTHER: I didn't hear the car ...

CHRIS: I left it in the garage.

MOTHER: Jim is out looking for you.

CHRIS: Mother ... I'm going away. There are a couple of firms in Cleveland, I think I can get a place. I mean, I'm going away for good. [*To* ANN *alone*] I know what you're thinking, Annie. It's true. I'm yellow. I was made yellow in this house because I suspected my father and I did nothing about it, but if I knew that night when I came home what I know now, he'd be in the district attorney's office by this time, and I'd have brought him there. Now if I look at him, all I'm able to do is cry.

MOTHER: What are you talking about? What else can you do?

CHRIS: I could jail him! I could jail him, if I were human any more. But I'm like everybody else now. I'm practical now. You made me practical.

MOTHER: But you have to be.

CHRIS: The cats in that alley are practical, the bums who ran away when we were fighting were practical. Only the dead ones weren't practical. But now I'm practical, and I spit on myself. I'm going away. I'm going now.

ANN [*going up to him*]: I'm coming with you.

CHRIS: No, Ann.

ANN: Chris, I don't ask you to do anything about Joe.

CHRIS: You do, you do.

ANN: I swear I never will.

CHRIS: In your heart you always will.

ANN: Then do what you have to do!

CHRIS: Do what? What is there to do? I've looked all night for a reason to make him suffer.

ANN: There's reason, there's reason!

CHRIS: What? Do I raise the dead when I put him behind bars? Then what'll I do it for? We used to shoot a man who acted like a dog, but honour was real there, you were protecting something. But here? This is the land of the great big dogs, you don't love a man here, you eat him! That's the principle; the only one we live by – it just happened to kill a few people this time, that's all. The world's that way, how can I take it out on him? What sense does that make? This is a zoo, a zoo!

ANN [*to* MOTHER]: You know what he's got to do! Tell him!

MOTHER: Let him go.

ANN: I won't let him go. You'll tell him what he's got to do ...

MOTHER: Annie!

ANN: Then I will!

[KELLER *enters from house.* CHRIS *sees him, goes down near arbour.*]

KELLER: What's the matter with you? I want to talk to you.

CHRIS: I've got nothing to say to you.

KELLER [*taking his arm*]: I want to talk to you!

CHRIS [*pulling violently away from him*]: Don't do that, Dad.
I'm going to hurt you if you do that. There's nothing to say,
so say it quick.

KELLER: Exactly what's the matter? What's the matter? You
got too much money? Is that what bothers you?

CHRIS [*with an edge of sarcasm*]: It bothers me.

KELLER: If you can't get used to it, then throw it away. You
hear me? Take every cent and give it to charity, throw it in
the sewer. Does that settle it? In the sewer, that's all. You
think I'm kidding? I'm tellin' you what to do, if it's dirty
then burn it. It's your money, that's not my money. I'm a
dead man, I'm an old dead man, nothing's mine. Well, talk
to me! What do you want to do!

CHRIS: It's not what I want to do. It's what you want to do.

KELLER: What should I want to do? [CHRIS *is silent.*] Jail?
You want me to go to jail? If you want me to go, say so!
Is that where I belong? Then tell me so! [*Slight pause.*]
What's the matter, why can't you tell me? [*Furiously*] You
say everything else to me, say that! [*Slight pause.*] I'll tell
you why you can't say it. Because you know I don't belong
there. Because you know! [*With growing emphasis and
passion, and a persistent tone of desperation*] Who worked for
nothin' in that war? When they work for nothin', I'll work
for nothin'. Did they ship a gun or a truck outa Detroit
before they got their price? Is that clean? It's dollars and
cents, nickels and dimes; war and peace, it's nickels and
dimes, what's clean? Half the goddam country is gotta go
if I go! That's why you can't tell me.

CHRIS: That's exactly why.

KELLER: Then ... why am *I* bad?

CHRIS: *I* know you're no worse than most men but I thought
you were better. I never saw you as a man. I saw you as my
father. [*Almost breaking*] I can't look at you this way, I
can't look at myself!

[*He turns away, unable to face* KELLER. ANN *goes quickly to* MOTHER, *takes letter from her and starts for* CHRIS. MOTHER *instantly rushes to intercept her.*]

MOTHER: Give me that!

ANN: He's going to read it! [*She thrusts letter into* CHRIS's *hand.*] Larry. He wrote it to me the day he died.

KELLER: Larry!

MOTHER: Chris, it's not for you. [*He starts to read.*] Joe ... go away ...

KELLER [*mystified, frightened*]: Why'd she say, Larry, what – ?

MOTHER [*desperately pushes him towards alley, glancing at* CHRIS]: Go to the street, Joe, go to the street! [*She comes down beside* KELLER.] Don't, Chris ... [*Pleading from her whole soul*] Don't tell him.

CHRIS [*quietly*]: Three and one half years ... talking, talking. Now you tell me what you must do. ... This is how he died, now tell me where you belong.

KELLER [*pleading*]: Chris, a man can't be a Jesus in this world!

CHRIS: I know all about the world. I know the whole crap story. Now listen to this, and tell me what a man's got to be! [*Reads.*] 'My dear Ann: ... ' You listening? He wrote this the day he died. Listen, don't cry. ... Listen! 'My dear Ann: It is impossible to put down the things I feel. But I've got to tell you something. Yesterday they flew in a load of papers from the States and I read about Dad and your father being convicted. I can't express myself. I can't tell you how I feel – I can't bear to live any more. Last night I circled the base for twenty minutes before I could bring myself in. How could he have done that? Every day three or four men never come back and he sits back there doing business. ... I don't know how to tell you what I feel. ... I can't face anybody. ... I'm going out on a mission in a few minutes. They'll probably report me missing. If they do, I want you to know that you mustn't wait for me. I tell you,

Ann, if I had him there now I could kill him – ' [KELLER *grabs letter from* CHRIS's *hand and reads it. After a long pause*] Now blame the world. Do you understand that letter?

KELLER [*speaking almost inaudibly*]: I think I do. Get the car. I'll put on my jacket. [*He turns and starts slowly for the house.* MOTHER *rushes to intercept him.*]

MOTHER: Why are you going? You'll sleep, why are you going?

KELLER: I can't sleep here. I'll feel better if I go.

MOTHER: You're so foolish. Larry was your son too, wasn't he? You know he'd never tell you to do this.

KELLER [*looking at letter in his hand*]: Then what is this if it isn't telling me? Sure, he was my son. But I think to him they were all my sons. And I guess they were, I guess they were. I'll be right down. [*Exits into house.*]

MOTHER [*to* CHRIS, *with determination*]: You're not going to take him!

CHRIS: I'm taking him.

MOTHER: It's up to you, if you tell him to stay he'll stay. Go and tell him!

CHRIS: Nobody could stop him now.

MOTHER: You'll stop him! How long will he live in prison? Are you trying to kill him?

CHRIS [*holding out letter*]: I thought you read this!

MOTHER [*of Larry, the letter*]: The war is over! Didn't you hear? It's over!

CHRIS: Then what was Larry to you? A stone that fell into the water? It's not enough for him to be sorry. Larry didn't kill himself to make you and Dad sorry.

MOTHER: What more can we be!

CHRIS: You can be better! Once and for all you can know there's a universe of people outside and you're responsible to it, and unless you know that, you threw away your son because that's why he died.

[*A shot is heard in the house. They stand frozen for a brief second.* CHRIS *starts for porch, pauses a step, turns to* ANN.]

CHRIS: Find Jim! [*He goes on into the house and* ANN *runs up driveway.* MOTHER *stands alone, transfixed.*]

MOTHER [*softly, almost moaning*]: Joe ... Joe ... Joe ... Joe ... [CHRIS *comes out of house, down to* MOTHER'*s arms.*]

CHRIS [*almost crying*]: Mother, I didn't mean to –

MOTHER: Don't dear. Don't take it on yourself. Forget now. Live. [CHRIS *stirs as if to answer.*] Shhh ... [*She puts his arms down gently and moves towards porch.*] Shhh ... [*As she reaches porch steps she begins sobbing.*]

CURTAIN

MORE ABOUT PENGUINS
AND PELICANS

Penguinews, which appears every month, contains details of all the new books issued by Penguins as they are published. From time to time it is supplemented by *Penguins in Print*, which is our complete list of almost 5,000 titles.

A specimen copy of *Penguinews* will be sent to you free on request. Please write to Dept EP, Penguin Books Ltd, Harmondsworth, Middlesex, for your copy.

In the U.S.A.: For a complete list of books available from Penguins in the United States write to Dept CS, Penguin Books, 625 Madison Avenue, New York, New York 10022.

In Canada: For a complete list of books available from Penguins in Canada write to Penguin Books Canada Ltd, 41 Steelcase Road West, Markham, Ontario.

ARTHUR MILLER

DEATH OF A SALESMAN

Death of a Salesman was written in six weeks in the spring of 1948, but it had been brewing in Miller's mind for ten years. Its 742 performances put it among the 50 longest recorded Broadway runs; it received the Pulitzer Prize for Theatre and was later filmed. Miller himself defined his aim in the play as being 'to set forth what happens when a man does not have a grip on the forces of life'.

NEW AMERICAN DRAMA

Edward Albee   The American Dream
Jack Richardson   Gallows Humour
Murray Schisgal   The Typists
Arthur Miller   Incident at Vichy

The four plays in this volume represent in their different ways the best of the new theatre of America. Edward Albee, author of *Who's Afraid of Virginia Woolf?*, has already made a considerable impact as one of the most exciting dramatists to appear in recent years. Murray Schisgal has won admiration from critics on both sides of the Atlantic, and Jack Richardson is beginning to be recognized as an important and highly original theatrical talent. Even Arthur Miller, established figure though he is, has made, in *Incident at Vichy*, a new and thoughtful departure that represents an important addition to his works.

NOT FOR SALE IN THE U.S.A.

Modern American Plays

THE CRUCIBLE

First performed in 1952, *The Crucible* may reasonably be described as one of the profoundest plays of the post-war world – a classic of the modern stage. It is the first, and so far the only, American play to be performed at the National Theatre.

The play's retelling of the story of the Salem witches had, at the time of its first production, a frightening relevance to the contemporary events of McCarthyism. Now that the immediate political message has faded, a more permanent dramatic force can be seen in Arthur Miller's drama.